May God continue
to bless & empower
you as you read & enjoy
this book.

Love,
[signature]

Unless otherwise indicated, all Old and New Testament Scriptures quotations are taken from the *New King James Version* of the Bible.

Scriptures quotations marked KJV are taken from the *King James Version* of the Bible.

Unless otherwise indicated, all Old and New Testament Scriptures quotations are taken from the *Amplified Bible*.

Manuscript and Project
By Veronica M. Williams, Ph.D.
Front and Back Cover Design
By Flo's Productions
Website: http://flosproductions.nstemp.biz
Email: florencedyer@comcast.net
810.624.3660

ISBN 0-9769645-1-1

TIME SOMEBODY TOLD ME

TIME SOMEBODY TOLD ME

BY

VERONICA M.WILLIAMS, Ph.D.

FLO'S PRODUCTIONS PUBLISHING SERVICE
An Affiliate of Writers & Self Publishers Association

WSPA
Writers and Self Publisher's Association

Genesee County

TIME SOMEBODY TOLD ME

A Word From The Publisher

I've had the distinct pleasure of knowing Dr. Veronica Williams for almost two decades. Dr. Williams is a strong virtuous woman of faith and power. It was truly an honor for me to be given the opportunity to publish *Time Somebody Told Me*. *Time Somebody Told Me* is a must have inspirational novel no woman should be without. Every woman who comes in contact with this dynamic book will be truly blessed.

–Florence Dyer
Owner of FLO'S PRODUCTIONS
Author/Publisher/Graphic Designer

Table Of Contents

TIME SOMEBODY TOLD ME

TIME SOMEBODY TOLD ME
That I am Lovely, Good and Real
That my beauty could make hearts stand still;

IT'S TIME SOMEBODY TOLD ME
That my love is total and so complete
That my mind is quick and full of wit
That my loving is just too good to quit;

TIME SOMEBODY TOLD ME

TIME SOMEBODY TOLD ME
How much they want, love and need me
How my spirit helps set them free
How my eyes shine full of the white light
How good it feels just to hold me tight;

TIME SOMEBODY TOLD ME
So I had a talk with myself
Just me-nobody else
Cause it was TIME SOMEBODY TOLD ME.

Author unknown

TIME SOMEBODY TOLD ME

Dedication

I dedicate this book to my mother, the late Margie Reagan Myres, a strong African-American woman, who taught me never to give up and to always believe in myself; who introduced me to Jesus Christ at a very young age; who showed me by example what a true Christian was; who read the entire Bible from cover to cover several times each and every year; who when she prayed, knew how to touch Heaven and miracles took place; who taught me what a lady looks like and acts like; who never stopped being proud of me and who was my best friend and the wind beneath my wings.

I dedicate this book also, with great admiration and love to the late Mother Etta Brown, Aunt Vera Vance and long time friend, Jacqueline Robinson. Their wisdom, strength, wit, quickness of perception and discernment always encouraged me, but their passing left me way too soon. To Odessa Mae Wiley, Margaret, Sheila, Sandra, Yolanda, Veronica H., Eraina, my daughters, Nicole, Jennifer, and Erica, and especially to my sister, Beverly Myres Brock, who is the perfect example of a wife and mother; and to those women who shaped and who continue to shape my life, both past and present, I dedicate this book to you.

VERONICA WILLIAMS, Ph.D.

Acknowledgements

I thank the Lord Jesus for giving me the push to write this book, for first speaking to me through my former Pastor, Timothy R. Stokes, whom I will always admire and respect. And later through several other prophets, whose prophetic words, continued to encourage me, to finish.

It is my desire that this book bring glory and honor to God, as women everywhere-----------adolescent women, teenage women, young adult women, older women, single women, and married women, read it and are set free.

Special thanks to my daughters, Nicole, Jennifer, and Erica who motivated me to be strong and keep going when everything in me wanted to give up.

Special appreciation to Teneka Thompson, Arlesia Fields, Nicole Williams, Jennifer Smiley, and my good friend, Rev. Marvin A. Jennings who were my proofreaders; your hours of dedication and tireless effort has helped to make this project a success. I would not have been able to do it without your help and labor of love.

Particular praise and recognition is given to my former Pastor's wife, Co-Pastor Tanya Stokes, whose integrity, sincerity, dedication, commitment, and wisdom far exceed her chronological age. She is a role model to women of leadership, scholarship, friendship, and faith. Thank you for your continued encouragement, time, and insightful contributions to my life.

Recognition is given to my present pastor, Bishop Robert E. Joyce, whose prophetic gift and insight far excels anyone I have ever encounter.

Special appreciation to my grandchildren, Taylor, Kevin Jr., Justin, and Kaiyah, who loves me unconditionally and who shares me reluctantly with the rest of my world. Grandmother loves you so very much.

Forward

Have you ever wondered why you've ended up disappointed or broken hearted in romantic relationships? Is it that "all men are dogs" or "all the good ones are taken" or "the ones who aren't married are in jail or gay." Well, it's time somebody told women that the power is not in their circumstances and there are ways to regain their power. It's time somebody told women that they *can* make choices to strengthen their mind, soul and spirit. It's time somebody let women know that you don't have to settle for poor treatment…that you should expect the best from others and from yourself. In *"Time Somebody Told Me"* therapist Veronica Williams gives you a step-by-step guide to self-empowerment. Unlike many of the books that inspire you for the moment, but give no practical advice, *"Time Somebody Told Me"* provides a step-by-step in-depth guide to help you improve your life and your relationships. Through reading this book you'll clearly see that Williams is a highly trained and educated professional therapist, however you will also feel her warmth. Williams comes across like a loving big sister, a best friend or a wise grandma, who's looking out for your best interest. Tell your sister, your friend, your mom, your daughter…anyone you care about to pick up their own copy so they can refer to it again and again. Read, take notes, and tuck Williams' pearls of wisdom away in your mind and heart. It's time to take that bold step toward the peace, joy and happiness you deserve. It's time for a book like this. It's *"Time Somebody Told Me."*

Arlesia Fields, MA, MBA
Broadcast Journalist

VERONICA WILLIAMS, Ph.D.

Introduction

Several years ago I received an urged call from a counselor at General Motors Employee Assistance Program. A GM employee was in his office, extremely depressed, and suicidal. The woman, whom I will call Edith, was refusing to go to the hospital as they had suggested, but had agreed to talk with me. They asked if I could see her right away on an emergency basis.

When Edith arrived, she thanked me for seeing her on such short notice. She was polite and stated that the only reason she had come was because she had promised the counselor that she would, however, her mind was made up, she had everything in order, and had planned to end her life that night. Her only mistake was in saying good-bye to a friend, which landed her in the counselor's office.

Edith began by stating that she couldn't understand why God had allowed her to live. Obviously she had been a mistake and she thought she should have never been born. She told me of an awful childhood in which her mother had been emotionally & physically abusive and rejecting. She stated her mother's male friends always came first, even when she told her that one had raped her at the age of ten years old.

Her mother sent her away instead of pressing charges against her lover. Edith related she didn't even care that much because her mother was sending her to the only person who had ever showed her love, her father. By now, her father had remarried and was living in another state. Right away, there was trouble between she and her stepmother. When her father left for work, her stepmother would beat her. One day, she told her father what was happening, even though she had been threaten that something terrible would happen if she did tell. Her father and stepmother got into a big argument, one thing led to another, and before she knew what was happening, her stepmother pulled a gun, fatedly wounding her father. She stood helplessly by, afraid to move, afraid to cry out. When she could move, she saw her father's blood flowing like a river under her feet. Her stepmother ran, never to be seen again.

Edith was returned to her mother's home. For the first time, she felt alone in this world and made several unsuccessful attempts at suicide. The hospital strongly suggested to the mother that she get Edith into counseling, but Edith refused to talk to her assigned therapist. Finally, they gave up and stopped attending.

By then she was a teen-ager and fell in love for the first time in her life. Her boyfriend would walk her home everyday and for the first time in a long time, she was happy. Then one day she came home from school to find her boyfriend in the bed with her mother. Her mother had seduced him as he waited for Edith to arrive home from cheerleading practice. She ran away from home. She never told her boyfriend that she was carrying his child until years later. She finally moved to Michigan to live with her grandmother and it was there that she finished high school. A year later, she got a job in one of the GM factories and met the man she would later marry.

Initially she thought, she would finally have a chance at true happiness, only to find that her husband was a batterer and just as emotionally abusive as her mother. They soon had a child, and her husband did all he could as their son was growing up, to turn her son against her. Things got so bad that her daughter, by her childhood sweetheart, left home.

Years later, her husband was diagnosed with cancer, and became bedridden. She waited on him hand and foot while still taking the verbal abuse. When he finally realized that he was not going to make it, he apologized for how he had treated her all those years, but never said why he did it.

Edith was suffering from Major Depression with a Borderline Personality Disorder, and had never been properly diagnosed. I was able to get her on the right medication and with insight and supportive psychotherapy, she began to improve. We took it a day at a time; she was at least living, and making better choices for herself by beginning to see that she had worth and that God had not made a mistake when she was born as she had previously thought.

Her daughter whom she loved and adored had married and lived in a nearby state. Her daughter had graduated from college and had done well. Edith felt that her daughter was the only thing she had that represented she had done something right. By now, Edith was a proud grandmother of two beautiful grandsons. They had kept her going when she had previously wanted to give up. Then one day, she received a frantic call from her daughter's husband to rush there as quickly as possible. Apparently her daughter had collapsed and they had rushed her to the hospital. Within two days, her 25-year-old daughter was dead. She called me from the hospital screaming and crying uncontrollably. Her daughter, whom I had met on several occasions, and who thanked me time and time again for saving her mother's life, had died from some rare disease that no one knew she had.

I was in shock. My heart went out to her. What more could this woman take? I prayed to God to please comfort her and to let her know and feel His Divine Presence.

It's been ten years since that call, and Edith is still here. She's stronger than she thought. Each day is a struggle, but each day is a victory also. Today, she is happy and enjoying her grandchildren. Her relationship with her son has been restored. Her mother became a born-again Christian and their relationship was restored before her mother died. We have cried together, laughed together, and prayed together. She is no longer in therapy, but she is always in my thoughts and prayers. It is for Edith and many women like her who has gone through insurmountable pain at the hands of people who was suppose to love them, that I write this book. It is time somebody told them of who they really are, of how wonderful they really are, of how strong they really are, and how beautiful they really are. It's time somebody told them that God didn't make a mistake when they were born, but instead, masterfully created such a unique individual that none other can compare to them.

In 30 years of during psychotherapy, I have treated thousands of women. Most of these women were intellectually astute, capable, educated, talented and beautiful. Many were professionals who had done extremely well for themselves in their chosen fields. But despite the fact that they could run successful businesses, make powerful decisions on a daily basis or lead organizations, train and teach children to be future leaders and hold families together; they lacked in one area.

They knew who they were publicly, who their families, friends, and co-workers thought they were, but most of them didn't really know for themselves, who they really were and this was most transparent in that one area where they were most vulnerable, their relationships with men. These women were like putty in the hands of a skilled sculptor. I have seen strong women who have it all together, fall apart and lose it due to the mistreatment of the man she was involved with. It may be an unfaithful husband boyfriend, or significant other, but eventually these women sit tearfully in my office and ask, "what's wrong with me; why does he treat me like this?"

The correct question I always answer, is not why does he treat you like this, but more importantly, "why do you allow it?"

Most women in these situations allow it because of fear, especially the fear of rejection. Rejection hurts so much that just the threat of it convinces most women to cooperate with their enemies. And many times, that enemy may be sharing your very own bed. By illuminating key patterns to sex and intimacy, I help these women see themselves for the very first time and empower them to break the destructive patterns that keep them captives and keep them in bondage.

I help them see the real truth. For you see, there are two types of truths—received truth and revealed truth. You can receive a truth and it can just become factual data or knowledge, but revealed truth is the only truth that will become your reality, which in turn will change your life. Knowing something intellectually and accepting it emotionally are two very different things.

"Time Somebody Told Me" allows the reader to experience the revelation it takes for a change that's truly life altering. In years of doing psychotherapy, I have used these approaches to not only help myself, but help other women as well. Helping women know who they really are by understanding the full range of their choices enables them to be more effective in every area of their life. Not recognizing your options is quite different from not having any options at all.

Women receive these truths and change their lives. They are based on unsurpassed clinical expertise and sound biblical principals. For who better knows a thing, or a person, or a woman, than the creator of it.

It's time for a book like this, it's *"Time Somebody Told Me"*.

--Veronica Williams

TIME SOMEBODY TOLD ME

I
"THE POWER WITHIN"

There is a dynamic power that is set free whenever we focus on the positive forces in life. It's a principle that every great achievement is based on. Knowing who you are, who you really are, will not only enable you to tap into this dynamic power, but will give you insight into the wisdom God has placed in you to accomplish anything in life you desire to do.

In their quest for identity, women often struggle through numerous stages of development whether it's physical, emotional, sexual or intellectual as they search to know who they really are. Low self-esteem, years of abuse, past hurts and pains, and negative self-talk keep negative images before them which do not allow them to break forth into the women of destiny that God has foreordained them to be. When you are able to change your thoughts based on God's word of who you are, then and only then will you be able to take dominion over every circumstance that would keep you bound in the negative arenas of life.

Simply put, right thinking, based on the right principles, is the means to an exciting, beautiful, and fulfilled life. I am a great proponent of the "power of positive thinking". I believe that there is truth to the concept of self-fulfilling prophecy. Thinking positive of ourselves leads to us experiencing positive living. The more negatively we feel about ourselves, the more we tend to filter out whatever positive feedback that comes from others. We will encounter enough enemies in our lives, we should not become one to ourselves. Remember the story of the little engine, " I think I can, I think I can, I think I can." Well, you can. You have all the tools you need inside of you to accomplish any task you desire to complete, to fulfill the destiny God set for you before the beginning of time.

It seems so often that unhappy, depressed, anxious, and unproductive people are not the victims of their circumstances, as they would like to believe, but rather the prisoners of their own negative thinking, and this is especially true for some women. Many are discouraged, lack courage, and are trapped by a fear of failure because they focus on the negatives of life.

Women in particular seem to be caught in a dilemma of needing a man to affirm them or not knowing how to affirm themselves. When you begin to affirm yourself and focus on your possibilities instead of focusing on your problems, you will begin to unlock enough energy and feelings of worth, self-confidence, and self-esteem within you to accomplish any task you desire to accomplish. These qualities I believe, are the necessary ingredients for success. **Personally, I believe in success, simply because the alternative is failure.** I also believe in success because when we succeed, other people are encouraged and challenged by our success to do great things in their lives.

We must always realize that we have a choice in life. The Bible says, "choose ye this day whom ye will serve." Some women choose a mate, then complain that he's lazy, won't work, unaffectionate and refuses to listen, won't spend any time with them, and is even unfaithful. Yet in a world of millions, he was your number one choice to pour your life into.

Somehow, it never occurs to us to assume responsibility for our choices …to look into the mirror and admit that many times we are using the wrong criteria to make the wrong choices.

Someone once said that, "you will not find right people in wrong places, good people in bad places, or pure people in impure places." And that's true. You don't go to the bar to find your mate in life. Yet countless of many men and women think that the bar is an acceptable meeting place to find a life partner.

It has also been said that opposites attract. You must keep in mind that **when dating someone, you must learn to ask yourself some very important questions, some honest questions, and some revealing questions.** Several years ago, one of my patients brought her fiancé to my office for me to meet. In the course of our conversation, he revealed that this would be his third marriage. He further shared with me that his first wife had died and his second marriage had failed because of mistakes he had made. Later when I talked to my patient alone, she did not know how his first wife died, how long his second marriage had lasted, nor how, he was to blame for the break-up of his second marriage. Many times girls who are raised in the church find worldly men fascinating, exciting, cool and suave. I don't care how exciting and different he is; **never ever bond with a rebel. Rebels are those who find themselves in a position against authority;** especially those who find themselves in a position against God's authority. This particular man had a history of drug use, and although he was now attending church with her, he had not yet kicked his habit. The Bible clearly tells us not to be "unequally yoked;" yoked or joined together with a non-believer, a non-Christian, and one who has different values, just for starters. When you bond with a rebel, you are forever welded to the future disasters he has scheduled in his life. And we both discovered later that he had many future disasters scheduled, but she wouldn't listen and was also welded to those disasters.

Far too many women settle for bad relationships because they don't know who they are. They settle for broken promises, distorted images of themselves, because they don't know who they are. Many settle for unfulfilling compromises because they don't know who they are. They allow someone else's view of them to determine their destiny. Many are caught in a cycle of abuse, whether it's emotional, physical, or sexual because they don't know whom they really are.

God said you are marvelous and wonderfully made. Do you understand what that really means? In Genesis 1:1-25, we see that God created the heavens and the earth. He created everything needed in the earth to sustain it. And God said that it was good. Then in vs.27, He created man. But when it came to the woman, God took one of Adam's ribs and skillfully **formed** woman. One definition of formed is "the structure of a work of art." You are skillfully made. **No other creature on earth was designed like you.** You were designed, molded, sculptured, and delicately made by the hands of almighty God. That's why you can be strong and yet tender, fragile, yet have the strength to hold families and nations together. Through you, generations are born. You nurture children and through your wisdom, give them a view of themselves to become leaders. **You are woman. Phenomenal woman, that's you.** You must learn to see yourself that way. But unfortunately, many women are blinded by the distorted views of others. Constantly, seeing themselves in a negatively light. Never being satisfied with who they are and who God formed them to be.

It's time to know who you are, to see you the way God sees you. To walk proud and not bowed down. To stand with dignity and grace in the knowledge of who God says you are. To talk and walk with confidence, assurance and pride. It's time to stop talking negatively about you. It's time to stop allowing others to put you down. It's time to stop the pity parties (no one attends them anyway) and the victim mentality way of thinking. It's time to look into the mirror and see the real you, not the lie that's been told you, but the real you.

For you see, the real you, is that one on the inside waiting to break forth or waiting to exhale. But she can't come forth until you unlock the door and allow her to break through.

Just like four thousand years ago when God led his chosen people out of bondage because of his great love for them. True to his nature, he wanted only good for them. He wanted them to possess all the liberty and joy he had to offer, yet the Israelites insisted on clinging to deaf and dumb idols made of stone and wood.

Today, we are faced with the same basic situations, clinging to the abusive and unfulfilled relationships that continue to keep us bound in those relationships, due to low self-esteem and victim personalities, especially a victim mentality. – a victim way of thinking.

I have spent my life and professional career seeking wholeness for other women and myself. What you will experience in the next chapters will secure your wholeness as well, and show you finally, how to exhale and finally let go and let God show you how to be all he has predestined you to be.

II
"WAITING TO EXHALE"

I remember clearly the day I unlocked the door to free my soul, to free the real me on the inside, that spirit me which is made in the image of God, my creator. The "me" that will not allow limits to be placed on me, that me who finally answered the call to fulfill my destiny.

For years I had been in an awful, abusive marriage. I didn't know then, that the Bible warns you not to be unequally yoked. I know now of course, that you should never marry someone who has different values from you, thinking you are going to change them. It will never work. As I look back now, I was just like so many teenage girls today, thinking my parents did not know anything when they told me, "He's not for you".

My ex-husband had come from the other side of town. His parents separated when he was in high school, because of years of womanizing that had been generationally handed down. **You must consider well the mentors of your mate.** What did his father teach him? What did his mother teach him? What philosophy had been branded into his conscience? Who was his spiritual oasis in his time of emptiness? To whom does he go to when there is great temptation in his personal life? Who advises him when crisis occurs? If, and when you consider these factors while you are dating, it can eliminate a whole lot of chaos later in your life. If I had known back then, what I know now, my life would have been so different. But I have learned to see God in everything and know that in everything He can turn it around and make it turn out better for our good. I believe now that if I had not gone through these experiences, there would not be this book to help you avoid some of the mistakes I made and the mistakes many women have made, thinking they were in love.

My ex-husband's father worked on the railroad and his mother worked for years as a domestic in a very affluent section of town. Although neither of his parents had a formal education they wanted the best for their children, and had provided well for them. His older sister, the first in the family to graduate from college had married well and she and her husband were quite successful in another state.

My ex-husband had graduated from Notre Dame Catholic High School, which was a very prestigious private school in town. To attend that school meant you were in the elite. I always wanted to attend, but my father was a proud man who believed in public education and since he had spent all his life working in public education, he said it would be an insult to have his children attend a catholic high school. So my initial impression of my ex-husband was false. I initially thought since he had graduated from Notre Dame that he had the same values I had grown up with. However, I later discovered that he had been kicked out of the public schools, and the only school that he was eligible to attend was a private one that he had to pay for. (Remember what I said about bonding with a rebel).

I had grown up as the eldest daughter, but the fourth oldest of six children. My three older brothers were quite a bit older than I, in fact being seven, eight, and ten years older. Both of my parents had a master's degree plus 30 hours above their masters. Education was a strong value in our home and had been for several generations. All of my siblings attended college with three of us completing masters, plus 30-degree programs. My aunts, uncles, even my grandfather had all attended and graduated from various universities.

When I met my ex-husband, he was very tall, handsome, and popular. I was in the 10th grade. He had graduated from high school and was preparing to go off to college. Our first real date was actually two years later when he was my escort at the "Debutante Ball". That was an important event in the south. That was the night that a young girl was formally introduced into society. She had been watched and studied carefully for years to see if she exemplified the high moral standards, behaviors, and academic excellence it took to be chosen to be a debutante. It was the formal event of the year. All through my teen years we were reminded that we couldn't do certain things or be out past a certain hour for fear you would not be chosen to be a debutante. If you were chosen, you would receive a formal letter in the mail stating you had been selected and had met the high standards needed to receive such an honor. I was so excited because I had never been out of my house at 12 o'clock midnight, which was when the ball ended. My ex, who was quite worldly, was fascinated with my naivete. All the girls he had previously dated could go to clubs and parties with him, but he could only see me on Sunday afternoons. He would later tell his friends that if he stayed too long at my house, my father would get up and walk through the living room with his hat and pajamas on, sending the strong message that it was time to go.

By then, my ex was a sophomore at Grambling State University in Grambling, Louisiana. After graduating with honors, I went off to Southern University in Baton Rouge, Louisiana. That summer he moved to Michigan and got a job with General Motors. He never returned to school. During the next four years that we were away from each other, we both changed. I was developing and maturing, no longer that shy little naïve girl, who depended on my ex to take care of me. We would only see each other maybe twice a year during those years, but our phone bill was outlandish. However, that didn't bother us because we always knew we would get married someday.

Peer pressure is so powerful. I understand what teens go through. You want to be like everyone else. My sophomore year,

I had integrated an all white university, Louisiana Tech, in Ruston, Louisiana. I had transferred from Southern University, which was a beautiful campus with a great history in Baton Rouge, La. Huey P. Long, the flamboyant governor of Louisiana from 1928 to 1932 had built Southern to be the largest and greatest black university in the south. Things were great for me there. I was Alpha Phi Omega Sweetheart and made friends that have lasted a lifetime. But one day in class, I knew I wasn't being challenged the way that I needed to be. I was making good grades with very little effort. I actually became afraid that one day I would need to help someone and I wouldn't know what to do. I needed to go someplace where I was not known and where I was not popular to challenge me to fulfill the potential that was within me. When I applied to Louisiana Tech and was accepted, I didn't know there were no other black students there. I hadn't even thought of it really. I had just assumed it was like any other school by that time. I mean, I assumed it was integrated. My senior year in high school was when the majority of schools in Shreveport had begun to integrate, even though schools were officially de-segregated in 1954 when a Supreme Court decision declared that all children, regardless of color, should have equal rights to a good education. For years they had gotten away with it in Shreveport by having an elementary and high school in every neighborhood. That way, it eliminated the need for bussing children across town to attend white schools that were not in their neighborhoods and integrating them.

By 1965, things had changed a lot in Shreveport. I had participated in many sit-ins and marches to end segregated lunch counters. My mother was frightened many nights while I was out picketing and marching. She later told me during those days, she stayed on her knees, but would have never told me not to do it, for she admired my courage and strength.

I discovered at Louisiana Tech that white girls acted quite different than my friends and I regarding dating. In fact, many of them had told me that they were at that university (which was the 3rd in the nation at that time in engineering) to get a husband, and

9

that their mother's had sent them there to get an engineer. And here I was, trying to get an education.

While at La. Tech, I even made history, being the first black student on their Student Government Association. I was Senior Women's Senator. I also fought to get jobs for black students who attended day classes, but didn't have enough money to stay on campus. I scheduled a meeting with the President of the university to discuss the problem. I told him that many of the black students had applied for financial aid and had been turned down, while the affluent white students had received work-study and various other jobs on campus. He not only gave my friends jobs, but gave me one as well, working in his office as student secretary to the President of Louisiana Tech University.

It was a big thing in the dormitory when a girl got pinned or engaged. All the girls were envious and would make a big deal out of the event. This is what I mean by peer pressure. For you see by now, I knew I didn't really love my ex, at least the way I saw these girls act in love, but I thought he loved me and that was all that mattered. To tell the truth, I didn't know what love was all about. I thought I was in love but just felt my ex loved me more. I had seen friends in high schools that were in love. Their boyfriends treated them badly. I had promised myself that I would never be treated that way, that I would marry someone who loved me more than I loved him. My ex and I became engaged my senior year. I remember calling my ex and telling him he could send my engagement ring, that I was ready for it now. For you see, the past year, whenever we were both home for a visit, he would try to get me to pick out an engagement ring. We were always looking in jewelry stores and I would always say that I was not quite ready. But now, because I wanted to be just like the other white girls in the dorm, and especially because I was the only black in the dorm, I was going to show them I could have a ring too if I wanted one. However, the closer it came to my graduation, the more I had this uneasiness in my spirit about my ex, but I ignored it. Our wedding was scheduled to be four days after my graduation. I remember questioning myself over and over, "should I do this?"

Integrating Louisiana Tech had been the toughest thing I had ever done so far in my life. I remember watching as a child, the television coverage of James Meredith who integrated OLE Miss University in Mississippi and the Little Rock nine, as they were the first to attend Central High School in Little Rock, Arkansas. I thought of how brave they were and how afraid they must have felt as they played a defining role in a major event that would mark a turning point in race relations in America. Little did I know then, that I would have a very similar experience as I integrated Louisiana Tech years later?

It was very lonely at first. I had been given a suite in the dormitory all to myself. White students would stare at me constantly. The only black faces I saw were the maids in the dormitory and the cafeteria workers that served our food. They were all so proud of me. They would see me on campus and bring me little gifts from their homes. Three other Black students were also enrolled, Lloyd, Liz, and Jackie. Soon other black students came, but we were only about four or five in a world of thousands. I remember feeling for the first time in my life what racism really felt like.

I had experienced something similar my senior year of high school. I was in the school band, playing the French horn. The football team and school band was preparing to go to Baton Rouge, La. to play in the state championship game. We were playing Saint Agustine, a huge catholic high school from New Orleans. President John F. Kennedy had just been shot and killed. My mother had taken me to the bank in downtown Shreveport to give me spending money for my trip. I watched in horror as many of the white people in the bank were laughing at the news and making racial remarks, like we finally got that "Nigger lover". The black people were crying and my mother was even afraid to let me go on the trip. I remember being afraid for the first time in my life because of racism. I couldn't understand how someone could hate like that. It was very frightening. My mother thought they would cancel the trip being we were playing a catholic high school and given the fact that President Kennedy was also a catholic.

We had been raised as an upper middle class family with both of my parents being very educated. All of my friend's parents were also educated and even though we didn't really associate with whites, it never mattered to us until we had to deal with injustices that someone encountered. Whites lived on their side of town and blacks lived on theirs. We had nice homes, nice cars, and all the things we needed. Those were happy days. They didn't bother us and we didn't bother them. If we were deprived of anything, we didn't know it. We even had instruments. My brothers, sister and I all played in the school band. Mother always saw to it that we had all the right lessons---piano, tap, ballet, choir, swimming, etc. So here I am, at Tech, facing racism head-on. I remember calling home and telling my mother, " I don't want to be here", that there were no other black kids here and I felt alone. She reminded me of who I was and who always walks besides me. I had been raised in the church, was very active in the church, and was even the Sunday school pianist and secretary. We would have church at home before we went to church on Sunday mornings by watching all the TV preachers. My mother had been prayer partners for years with Oral Roberts Ministry and had been to ORU several times. She said, "Veronica, you have always been a leader, you graduated with honors, was involved in many leadership positions throughout your school years, you have a good mind, you are strong and you can handle it. Hold your head up high and never allow anyone to look down on you. You have as much right to be there as anyone else." That was not what I wanted to hear. I wanted her to say that she and my daddy was coming to rescue their little girl. Not my mother, she was always pushing me to do more. She was truly, the wind beneath my wing.

Pretty soon, white girls started coming up to me speaking. A group came to my room one night and said, " you know what they call you on campus?" I said, "No". "They call you the Indian princess," someone said. I asked, "why"? " Well, you don't look black", another said. "You mean I don't fit your stereotype of what a black person should look or act like, I replied. Well, as I continued, "we come in all shades, shapes and sizes." "But you are different," they insisted. "No, I am not, I insisted. You need to learn that we are people just like you and we don't all look alike or act alike. Just as whites don't all look alike or act alike." My experiences at Tech will truly make another book; I only mention it to help you see where I was mentally at that time in my life. Well my ex sent my ring and that's how I became engaged. Really competing with the other white girls in the dorm to show them that I could have a ring too, if I wanted one.

Your spirit man is always trying to talk to you, trying to tell you "This is the way, walk ye in it". Even my body was trying to tell me, not to go through with it. In fact, the night of the wedding rehearsal, I became paralyzed with severe muscle spasms in my back and couldn't walk. I was confined to bed and they did the wedding rehearsal without me. That should not have surprised me because my girlfriends had planned most of the wedding without my participation. They were so excited that they had done it all. I got caught up in the excitement of it all, but still something was saying, "Don't do it". I felt obligated and was afraid or lacked the courage to change the course of things. Basically it was a soul-tie relationship. A soul-tie relationship is one where it looks like love, feels like love, but it's not love. It is an ungodly soul-tie. You are emotionally tied together and feel bound. You think because you have been together for so long, that you should remain together. My ex and I had dated for seven years, mostly apart. He was very controlling and jealous. He was abusive even then, being so jealous that he wanted to fight anyone that looked at me, in his perception, the wrong way. When I would complain, he would say that he just loved me so much. I didn't know that it was a sick relationship. As a therapist now, I can look back and see some of the classic signs that my ex was a potential batterer.

Signs to look for in a Battering Personality

Many people are interested in ways that they can predict whether they are about to become involved with someone who will be physically abusive. In some cases, a batterer may have only a couple of behaviors that the victim can recognize, but they are very exaggerated (e.g., **Extreme Jealousy** over ridiculous things). At the beginning of a relationship, an abuser will always say that his jealousy is a sign of love; **jealousy has nothing to do with love.** It's a sign of insecurity and possessiveness. **Controlling Behavior** is another sign. They try to control their partner's behavior, money, and ability to make choices. **Unrealistic Expectations** are another sign. The abuser is very dependent on their partner for all of their needs; they expect their partner to be the perfect wife, mother, lover and friend. The partner is expected to take care of everything for the batterer emotionally and in their home. (I didn't even realize until I divorced my ex years later, how much pressure I was always under).

Moodiness is another sign. An abuser's moods may change from sulking silently when upset, to having an explosive temper. Their moods may be totally unpredictable so that their partner and their children may be on guard at all times and feel as if they are walking on eggshells. This dual personality alternates from extreme tenderness to extreme aggressiveness. The moodiness may present itself as depression and at times be suicidal. They may even threaten suicide and tell their mate that it will be their fault if indeed suicide is committed. Another sign is **Isolation**. An abuser will try to cut their partner off from all resources, and will accuse people who are the victim's supports of "causing trouble." Many times they **blame others for their problems.** They will tell the partner that they are at fault for almost everything that goes wrong. They will criticize their partner and put her down to make themselves feel better. They are **hypersensitive**. The batterer is easily insulted. They claim their feelings are "hurt" when they're really angry, or take the slightest setbacks as personal attacks. Many times they are **cruel to children or animals**. This is a person who may punish animals brutally or is insensitive to their pain and suffering. They may expect children to be capable of doing things far beyond their ability. **"Playful" use of force in sex** is another sign. They may act out fantasies during sex where the partner is helpless. They are letting their partner know that the idea of "rape" excites them. They may start having sex with their

14

partner while they are sleeping, or demand sex when their partner is ill or tired. In addition to saying things that are meant to be cruel and hurtful, **verbal abuse,** can be seen by the abuser degrading the victim, cursing them, and running down any of their accomplishments. The abuser will tell their victim that they are stupid and unable to function without them. **Threats of violence** are always present. This would include any threat of physical force meant to control a partner. There are a few more signs, but I mention these because these are seen more frequently.

Now let's get back to my story, but really the story of many women who find themselves caught in this web and who may have been taught to be subordinate and submissive in their intimate relationships. It may be difficult to think of yourself as someone who has rights and who directs your own life, but you do and it can start now.

I was so immature in my thinking and really had no idea of what life was really all about. Mothers, we must prepare our daughters to be more than just scholars. We must prepare them for life. I just didn't have the courage, at the time, to say to my ex; "this is not going to work, and good-bye." Nor did I have courage to tell my family that they were right and I was wrong about him.

I have always been competitive. As I look back, I think the main reason I stayed in that relationship was the fact that everyone wanted him and I had him. He was an extremely good-looking man at that time that even white girls wanted to date him. Believe me, that is not a reason to be involved with anyone. But I mention it because so many young girls today get involved for all the wrong reasons, just as I did. Things like; "he's so fine and cute" and "he drives a nice car" are not reasons to get involved with someone you know little or nothing about.

Our wedding was beautiful, but I felt I was with a stranger. I never shared with anyone my feelings and fears. We left for Michigan a day or two after the wedding. Immediately, when we arrived in Michigan, I knew I didn't know this man, who was now my husband. It didn't matter that we had dated for seven years, mostly apart, I didn't know him. But I was soon to find out all about him.

My ex was just like his father, a womanizer. Women were calling constantly and he had lots of lies to justify his stories. I was still quite naïve. The first week we were married, he stayed out all night. I was terrified. Was he in an accident? Had he been killed? I felt so alone. I was in this strange city with no family and with a man I really didn't know. It was around 6am when I heard the door being unlocked. He reeked of alcohol and smoke. I hurled questions at him "where were you?" Why didn't you call?" Do you realize I was worried sick?" I continued to shout, telling him that I had called the police, hospitals, and every friend of his that I had met so far. He was furious and told me to never check up on him again. He couldn't understand why I would do something like that. I was totally disgusted and disappointed, but mostly hurt. I yelled that I never knew men who stayed out all night. My father and brothers had always come home. I had never been exposed to behavior like that before. I later discovered that this was   normal behavior for him.

Things didn't get any better; it just grew progressively worst. One thing that I learned during that period of my life was **"that it takes two people to make a relationship, but only one to change the quality of it"**.

My life was a living hell. He was insanely jealous. If I were a minute late, he would rant and rave, even accuse me of seeing someone else. I remember thinking; this man is crazy, I kept thinking I had to do something to make it better, that I had to fix it. I was too ashamed to call my mother and tell her she was right. I should have never married this man. If only my father was still alive, I kept thinking, he would rescue me.

My father died months before my wedding. He especially didn't like my ex and had objected to my dating him. But I had felt he didn't like my ex because he had come from the other side of town and I felt my father was being a bigot. All my life, even as a child, I had pulled for the underdog. I was the kid who brought home stray dogs and would pull for the Indians when watching westerns on television. I just knew that if my father were alive he would have stopped me from marrying him, and that would have been my way out.

One day though, I had had all the craziness I could take. We had had another argument as usual and I had run outside to get away from him. I would sometimes go sit in the backyard, go for a walk or go for a drive until I thought he had calmed down. This particular day when I came back, he had locked me out. Can you believe that? I became so furious that I scared myself. Something rose up on the inside of me and I literally kicked that door down. I thought, "this Negro is really crazy". He couldn't even qualify to get the house. It was my credit and my down payment that had got the house in the first place and he was going to lock me out of my own house. I don't think so. When he heard all the commotion, he came flying out of the bedroom to see what happened? When he saw what I had done, he was afraid to say a word. Actually I think he was in shock. I simply stepped over the debris and walked into my house.

Remember I said the real you, is the one on the inside that's waiting to break forth, but she can't until you unlock the door and allow her to come forth. Most of us have this view down deep inside of us of who we desperately want to be, of who we want to look like and act like. We get a glimpse of her every now and then, but we think that's so unattainable that we let it go. But that's the real you. Until you can change your present view of yourself that has been distorted by others through years of hurts and pains, the real you will remain locked up down deep on the inside waiting to exhale.

I had a patient tell me some years ago, that as I began to help her see who she really was, instead of the victim that she had allowed herself to become, she could visualize down deep inside, the real her. She could see "the real her" rise up to almost the top and slowly take a peek out, but she couldn't seem to climb all the way out.

She was a divorced mother of three children, living with her boyfriend who wasn't working. He was constantly putting her down and belittling her. She worked a full-time job and was going to college part-time. She stated her goal was to get a professional job and provide a better life for herself and her children. Her live-in boyfriend was constantly putting her down for pursuing her goals.

Sisters, when you finally get a picture of who you are, who you really are, there are things that you will refuse to tolerate any longer and a lot of garbage you'll leave behind.

I remember her saying, "Dr. Williams, I'm so tired of failing." "Failing at what?" I asked. "At relationships", she stated. "My first marriage ended in divorce because of abuse," and she didn't want to fail at another. I suggested to her that we take a closer look at this picture. I stated to her that she was a good mother who worked a full time job, plus was working on her degree so she could provide a better life for her children. I asked her if she felt she was in a successful relationship now. "You are involved with a man who puts you down, does not share your values or goals, who lives in your house, eats the food you provide, does not work or contribute anything to the household except babysitting while you are at work and school. And you are worried about this relationship failing. You are unhappy and miserable. Don't you think something is wrong with this picture?"

Women often ask me when they are in abusive "relationships, why does he treat me this way?" "Why does he do this?" I always answer with the same answer. **Why he does it, is not important. Why you allow it, is more important and is the only question that needs an answer.**

Iyanla Vanzant, in her book, "One Day My Soul Just Opened Up", called this insanity, and I agree. Not the insanity that gets you thrown into the loony bin, but the insanity where people stay in relationships where they cheat or are cheated on; where they remain in situations of all kinds where they are abused, neglected, demeaned, overlooked, and dehumanized; the insanity that makes you forget who walks besides you and who lives within you and that, as a result of this loss of memory, shuts down your soul.

If you or anyone you know show signs of these symptoms, beware! This person could be walking around convinced that he or she is fine. Most insane people do that, you know. Be aware that beneath the "everything is fine" exterior, there may be a malignant fungus of fear, confusion, and misery eating away at the soul. As the soul is eaten away, each day becomes a task of drudgery. The people in the environment become crutches and victims, or perceived oppressors. If you or anyone you know is in the midst of something or everything falling apart, take heed! This could be the first sign of insanity waiting for the opportunity to take over, cloud the mind, and destroy the spirit. If that happens, some part of you or someone you know is about to shut down. It must shut down in order for you to survive. If, on the other hand, you recognize these symptoms in yourself or someone you know, here is a piece of advice: " there is something bigger than you know going on here."

Many times we tend to overload ourselves, thinking we can handle stress after stress after stress. If we fail to take care of the problem, by seeking the help of a professional, for instance, the human body will take care of itself, by shutting down. Some have defined "nervous breakdowns" as just that, the body healing itself, shutting down because you didn't have enough sense to take care of you.

Life may sometimes seem to burden us with more than we can or want to bear. It's not that we cannot handle it. It is usually that we do not know how to handle it. We become angry many times when life hits us hard. Angry that we do not know what to do and angry with the ones who were suppose to teach us and didn't. Many women are angry with their mothers. Many men are angry with the fathers. And then there are those who are angry with both.

In order for a woman to love herself as a woman, her inner little girl needed to be loved by a woman. I'm not talking about sexual orientation. I'm talking about your very being. Much has been written about the failure in mothering that many people have experienced. This failure has a special impact on daughters. The failure in mothering is due mainly to the failure in marital intimacy. Because of this failure, the mother is frustrated and lonely. She may turn to her son and make him her little man, thus rejecting her daughter. Or she may turn to her daughter and use her to fill her emptiness. The daughter cannot be loved for herself in such an enmeshed situation. She has no mirroring that would allow her to develop a sense of self. She takes on the lonely, shame-based self of her mother, who is longing for her husband's love.

When a little girl does not have the healthy love of her mother, she grows up missing crucial aspects of her sexual identity. This is why so many women magically believe that they are adequate as women only if a man loves them. If their male relationship ends, they panic. They then rush into another male relationship in order to feel okay. If this sounds like you, you need to let your wounded inner child experience the love of a woman. Find two or three women who are willing to commit to being vulnerable with you. Don't try to do therapy with one another or fix one another; just be there to support one another in seeking self-actualization. Women already bond together on the basis of vulnerability. Too often the bond is common victimization. Your inner little girl needs to know that she can make it with you and your support group, that she does not need a man to be happy. She may want a man in her life as a part of her natural female drive for sexual love, male bonding and marriage. But she can achieve that best when she is self-sufficient and independent. For only when she is independent, can she enter into a relationship as a 100 percent, whole person.

I don't know where we get this 50/50 nonsense. Don't you know if you put 50 percent into a relationship that's all you are going to get out of the relationship, if that much?

My ex-husband and I separated several times during our fifteen-year marriage. I know God has really healed me, because I can't remember much of the abuse today. The fighting, even pulling a gun on me to keep me from leaving with our baby daughter is still vague. The temper tantrums and constant moodiness, never knowing what to expect when he came home, the walking on eggshells has all but been erased from my consciousness. But I can't make that statement for my daughters. It has not been erased from their consciousness, especially my two oldest girls. It affected how they relate to men and it has taken years of love and support to develop the inner healing they needed for their wholeness to take place. Through maturity, therapy, and spiritual growth on both their father's part and theirs, a whole new relationship has emerged. One that is loving, whole and healthy.

I remember going to my pastor back then, who is not my present pastor, seeking help. I needed him to tell me what to do from a spiritual point of view. I was a Christian, trying to do the right thing, but I felt like I was in hell. All he kept telling me to do was pray. I began to search the scriptures for myself. God had to show me a way out of this mess. I was doing all I knew to do, raising our daughters, three of them by now, practically alone; at least it felt that way.

Kay Marshall Storm's excellent book, " In the Name of Submission" deals in clear, tense language with one of the ugliest of abuses, wife battering. Without mentioning codependency by name she sets down very clearly, it's causes and effects, particularly on the children.

The Christian wife is taught that the husband is the head of the house, as Christ heads the church. So far, so good. There is no better formula for successful marriage than that found in scripture, and a tribe with two chiefs and no Indians won't function long. But when a man (whose father probably, according to the statistics, was also a wife-beater) promulgates an abusive relationship, he'll find plenty of false evidence in scripture to support his abuse.

It's not hard, in 1 Corinthians 7:4, he need only accept Paul's teaching that the husband rules over the wife's body, ignoring the rest of that verse, of course, that says the wife rules over the husband's body. In that same chapter, verse 10, Paul declares that a wife should not separate from her husband. Yet, how few women are counseled in the rest of that same verse-but if she does… Paul left the door open for extreme cases.

Ms. Strom counsels wisely that the abusive husband is almost never going to change unless the wife takes drastic steps to force a change. Separation with the ultimatum "you must undergo treatment before I will return" is just about the only successful means a wife has of easing the abuse. Are the children warped by a relationship in which the husband mistreats his wife? Every time.

The wife is called upon to be subject to her man (Ephesians 5:22), but hardly anyone notices that in 5:21 Paul has used exactly the same word to call every Christian into similar submission to one another. Neither is the wife-beater likely to take seriously Paul's admonition to husbands in Ephesians 5:25 to love the wife protectively and sacrificially.

Discipline? The abusive husband quotes Hebrews 12:7, which extols God's disciplining of his faithful, and twists it to suggest that the man ought to keep his mature adult wife in line in the same way one might discipline a small child, or God might discipline an errant saint. After all, everyone knows the wife's chief duty is to please her man (the I Corinthians 7:32-35 passage, so often used as a proof text, states just as firmly that the husband similarly should please his wife). Not only is divorce unthinkable, it is construed as trumpeting to the world that the wife somehow failed to make a happy home. Thus in marriage, but too often especially in Christian marriage, denominational interpretation and tradition, bind the woman to an unholy union of fear and pain.

Because of her erroneous concept of submission and her strong abhorrence of divorce or separation, the Christian wife may have little recourse but to take refuge in terrible denial. Most importantly, keep in mind that denial is the most powerful and harmful attitude you will ever fight within yourself and that no real healing can commence until it is set aside.

I knew my ex-husband had women and was having affairs; of course he was constantly denying it and I thought I had to catch him in order to validate my suspicions. Women were constantly calling my house and he would lie about the reasons. I saw in the word of God that He, meaning God, has called us to peace. My life was anything but peace. I saw where He said that He hated divorce, but that He allows it because of the hardness of men's heart. And if the unbeliever wanted to go, let him go. That the believer was not bound in a situation like that. Well, my ex-husband had left. Not physically, but emotionally, left as the head of the household, as the provider. So although he was still physically in the house, he had left the marriage covenant.

The marriage covenant is a powerful thing and when it is broken by adultery and physically abuses, God does not expect you to remain in a relationship where your life is in danger and the life of your children is being emotionally damaged. I knew that I had done all I could to save this marriage, so when I decided to leave, I left without any guilt.

I quit my job and moved back to Louisiana. One of my high school friends who was now a successful attorney handled my divorce and my daughters and I settled into our new life in Louisiana. My ex never let go. He would call constantly, sometimes even up to fifteen times a day, begging and pleading for me to give him another chance, for me to come back. When I was not there, he was calling and working on the children, trying to lay a guilt trip on them for not convincing me to return. This was especially hard on my oldest daughter, who he did the most emotional damage too. Thank God she is great now, but woe to the man that got in her way years earlier. She wasn't taking anything off of any man. She was hard and tough and that toughness ruined several relationships for her.

Never settle for half of anything, especially in a relationship. I remember the day when my ex-husband had run out of things to say to convince me to come back. He cited all the reasons that even he couldn't deny anymore of why I should never come back. Then he said that, "half a man was better than no man at all", and I should come back for that reason alone, if nothing else. I can't even put into print how I responded to that lie from the pit of hell. Please somebody tell me how can half of anything be better than a whole? What is more surprising to me is that many women have told me that same exact lie. Somehow, due to their low self-esteem, they have bought the lie that you need a man, and it doesn't matter what kind of man, only that you need one to affirm you as a woman.

I just love what the serenity prayer states, "God, grant me the serenity to accept the things I cannot change, the courage to change the things I can and the wisdom, Almighty God, to know the difference." Thank you Jesus, I knew the difference. Thank you Jesus, my self-esteem was developed enough through years of hard struggle, to walk away from that hell.

When you don't know who you are, you will often allow someone else's image of you to shape your image of yourself. Sometimes we hinder ourselves by focusing our attention in the wrong direction. Too often we search for the answers to life's riddles in the external world. We are forever looking outside ourselves, seeking approval and striving to impress others. But living to please others is a poor substitute for self-love, for no matter how family and friends may adore us, they can never satisfy our visceral need to love and honor ourselves.

Making our needs, our first priority is difficult for all of us, but it is particularly challenging for women. Early on women learn that we are born to serve, that the needs of others supersede our own. We are taught that sacrifice and selflessness are virtues that make us worthy and win us love. Although charity is an expression of divinity, it is a human virtue also, and not the reserve or obligation of women alone. Whether we are female or male, we must not allow the relentless demands of family and work to override our critical need for self-nurturing. When we fail to nurture ourselves, our joy is depleted and our capacity to serve diminished. Giving from an empty vessel causes stress, anger and resentment, seeds that sow disorder and disease. Attempting to meet the needs is an act of self-betrayal that can cause us to lose respect for our value and worth. It is not enough to be kind: **we must learn to be kind and wise.**

Living in balance is vital to our well being. Without balance, much of the beauty and grandeur of our existence is lost. But a balanced life doesn't just happen. It is a state of grace we create by staying connected with our thoughts, and feelings, and consciously measuring what we do. Just as feeling fit and flexible demands physical exercise, just as expanding your mind requires intellectual effort, so bringing your life into balance and maintaining your spiritual equilibrium require focused awareness and daily retreat from the stresses of the world.

You must learn that the wisdom and strength that you seek awaits you in your inner man. As you look to the light that is within you, which was placed there by God, it is awaiting and longing for your return. You may have lost sight of your inner radiance as you turned to look outside yourself for validation and meaning. You may have forgotten it as you gave authority not to your own inner voice, but to the dictates and opinions of others. Yet no matter how far you wander or how long you stay away, the divine light never flickers or dims. You are host to the eternal flame. It glows in the silence of your being, to illumine your life, light your way, and help you discover the real you. "…But if we walk in the light, as he is in the light, we have fellowship one with another, and the blood of Jesus Christ his son cleanses us from all sin." (1 John 1:7). He is always present in the person of the Holy Spirit to show you the light, which guides you in the right direction.

III
"THE JOURNEY FOR SELF"

How do we discover who we are? What road do we take to start this journey of discovery? When does it start? What is my purpose for being here? Why do I think the way I think? Why do I feel the way I feel? These are just a few of the questions we ask in our journey for self-discovery.

Due to our **Programming, Beliefs, Attitudes, Feelings and Behavior**, each one of us, has arrived at where we are today. Do you realize that our programming starts the minute we are born, with the way we are treated, spoken to, the things that are said, specific actions of people, reactions to our attempts to communicate, and much more. We begin to learn through what we are told and the way we are told. Unfortunately, most of what we hear about ourselves is negative. So we begin to program our minds with negative thoughts that lead to feelings of inadequacy, and those feelings of inadequacy, lead to negative behavior. Later on in life, we use this programming to make decisions, to analyze, to solve problems, to communicate and do many other things. Psychiatrists say, that by the time we are 16 years old, we have already been programmed with over 140,000 negative thoughts about ourselves, compared to just a few hundred positive thoughts about ourselves. Is it any wonder that we feel so inadequate?

Our programming then leads to our beliefs. Our beliefs are vital, because our ability to believe deeply about something is the core for all our attitudes. See it is not whether something is true or not, that is important, but whether or not we believe it to be true.

The Bible states, " as a man thinketh in his heart, so is he." Your thinking is always responsible for where you are. Every situation in your life is a result of how you are thinking. This is why God tells us to renew our minds with the word of God. Implantation of God's word can save your life and your soul. God has answers that will help you on a daily basis with the issues with which you struggle. No problem is bigger than God is, and many of His solutions for your life can be found in His word.

Your beliefs lead to your attitudes. Attitudes are really habits. Some **women do not really decide their future, they decide their habits, and then their habits decide their future**. Many times habits are automatic responses to certain stimuli. Attitudes are what you think, what you feel, and what you do in regard to anything. Attitudes can be positive or negative, with each leading to a different end. Attitudes can be changed also. Change is the greatest problem we face today. People don't like to change. Change is hard. John F. Kennedy once said, **"Change is the law of life. And those who look only to the past or the present are certain to miss the future."** People want to change their circumstances, but they do not want to change themselves. Women want to lose weight for example, but they don't want to change how they eat, nor get up early to exercise, or do whatever it takes to lead a disciplined lifestyle to bring about the change they desire. When you want something you have never had, you have to do something you have never done. You will never effect change in your life until you effect change in your attitude toward what is holding you back today.

Your attitude leads to your feelings or emotions. Empathy is listening to others to discover their feelings, and using leadership skills to lead others to action based on their emotions. Your feelings reflect how you "feel" about things in general. The more powerful your feelings are, the more you are motivated to reach your goals in relation to your feelings. This is because **motivation takes place through emotion, not logic**. The stronger the feelings, the more powerful the desire. Young girls may spend hours in front of the mirror trying to look their best because of the need or desire to be liked, accepted, and loved. Many women will starve themselves, even place their health in danger, thinking that will make them beautiful and desirable and land them "Mr. Right".

The outcome of anything you do is directly in proportion to the amount of desire with which you begin. For example, picture in your mind what you want to do. Next, write it down. Then begin to think about it every day and night. The desire that results will be all the motivation you will ever need. Next fan the fires of desire by reading your goals daily. Focus the goal in your mind and keep it there. The power of visualization will enable you to achieve success and accomplish any task. Women, let's make this simple, picture this "beautiful" dress you want. You especially want to wear it to this really nice affair with your man. You don't have the money for the dress, but you want it so badly that you can taste it. You can see yourself in it. You can even hear all the compliments you will receive when you walk through the door. The more you meditate on the dress, visualize yourself in the dress, you become overwhelmed with the desire that you have to have that dress. The more you meditate, the more creative you become to obtain it. Your motto becomes " by any means necessary, I am getting that dress". On the night of the affair, you walk in wearing that dress. It has become your reality because of your strong motivating desire.

No matter what you want, whether it's a beautiful dress or a beautiful home, build a burning desire for its accomplishments with your thought processes and it will be yours, given the appropriate action and time.

Feelings then lead to our behaviors. Behavior is the action initiated by feelings. Behavior is what one does. If the behavior needs to be changed, then the feelings, attitudes, beliefs, and programming all have to be taken into consideration. Behavior can best be changed through reprogramming or replacement of thoughts in our minds.

You are what you think. The Bible says it this way, **"as a man thinketh in his heart, so is he"**. You think about what you put into your mind through the process of repetition. No one just thinks of something once and they have it. But it is through repetitive thought that we believe and make it a reality in our life. So be careful what you think. Guard the door to your mind well. You are the guard, and only you can allow thoughts to enter your mind. You will eventually become what you think about the most, for the secret of your future is hidden in your daily routine or your daily habits, which is why you should never complain about what you permit. You hold your key to your future. Only you! Remember that you will never leave where you are, until you decide where you would rather be. Once you get that picture and began to act on it, nothing can hold you back except you.

The most important thing that you can learn is to "think positively". Life is merely an extension of what we think. What you think, you confess, and you then, experience. That which occupies the mind the majority of the time determines eventually, what you will become.

Life is merely a state of mind. Worry, tension, unhappiness, failure, loneliness, boredom, etc., are all a state of mind. So are success, recognition, achievement, love, growth, and security. All that man seeks is really a state of mind or being. Proper attitudes and right thinking achieve all the basic things people want from life. William James once said, "the greatest discovery of my generation is that human beings can change their lives by changing their attitudes." Charles Swindoll once stated on the subject of developing a positive attitude, that "the longer I live, the more I realize the impact of attitude on life. Attitude, to me is more important than facts. It is more important than the past, than education, than money, than circumstances, than failures, than successes, than what other people think or say or do. It is more important than appearance, giftedness or skill. It will make or break a company…A church…A home. The remarkable thing is we have a choice every day regarding the attitude we will embrace for that day. We cannot change our past…We cannot change the fact that people will act in a certain way. We cannot change the inevitable. The only thing we can do is play on the one string we have, and that is our attitude. I am convinced that life is 10% of what happens to me and 90% of how I react to it. And so it is with you…We are in charge of our attitudes."

Positive results in life are the direct results of positive thoughts. Negative results come from negative thoughts. These statements are very simple, but the system through which we function is much more complicated, that being the ' man mind. It is not by accident that God tells you to gu. ur mind. The mind is the most vital function of the human be ' is remarkably compact. The brain only weighs about 50 ounc the average adult male and about 5 ounces less in the female. 1 'res about 1/10 of one volt of electricity to perform its everyda 'tions. The brain is composed of tens of billions of nerve ce 'led neurons, each with a nerve ending. The neurons commun. 'hrough tiny gaps called synapses. There are trillions of t. 'apses, with a potential of retaining billions of bits of informa The brain can process up to 100 million bits of information pei Do you see why God said you are wonderfully made? We fu \, literally, at a level far beneath our true abilities.

The brain leaves the most advanced computers fai d in its truly staggering capacity. A modern computer, to be 'le of doing what the human brain can do, would have to be abu . 10,000 times larger than the average brain. Let me help you for a moment get a true picture of which you are and what a marvelous piece of machinery that God has designed---**you!**

The mind is made up of two parts, the conscious and the subconscious. Let's look at each part and try to understand how it works so you can use it more effectively. The reason I say this is because it's been said that we use only about one-tenth of your brain and the ones who have been fortunate enough to use another 10% are considered to be geniuses.

The Conscious Mind

The conscious mind is the one you know best because you have a reasonable amount of control over it. The conscious mind reasons, analyzes, calculates, makes determinations and decisions, makes judgements, and thinks and reacts. All are functions of the conscious mind and despite all of this, it can only deal with one thing at a time and be effective.

The Subconscious Mind

The powers of the subconscious mind are less obvious but far greater. In fact, the potentials of the subconscious are so vast that modern science can only speculate about what those capabilities might be. The subconscious controls motor functions, feelings, emotions, and stores our lifetime of knowledge and experiences. It uses information to satisfy the goals of the conscious mind. The subconscious can be influenced by the conscious mind. It will take suggestions from the conscious mind and act upon those suggestions and consider their directions. The subconscious does not care whether the suggestions are right or wrong, good or bad, positive or negative, it only fulfills its functions as a servant of its master, the conscious mind. The subconscious makes up about 88% of the mind. This means that you are aware of only 12% of the mind's activity. Isn't that phenomenal?

The subconscious can be compared to a **resource room**. Everything you have ever been exposed to, ever seen, every person you have ever met is all stored in the subconscious. The mind uses all of the information as a resource to deal with life. It has been estimated that about two million bits of information come into the central nervous system every second. You are not aware of all of this because they go to different parts of the brain where they are used automatically. All of this stored information and instructions have formed habit patterns. Since we are creatures of habit, most of what we do is automatic. This programming can be changed and controlled, but it operates until the day we die. Everything that has ever happened to you is stored in the subconscious and will remain there. It does not matter if the information is true or false, it is stored just the same.

If the subconscious is the resource room, then the conscious mind is the **guard** at the door. The guard very carefully sorts out information going to the subconscious. If it does not agree with it, then it is not taken to the resource room. That is why it is necessary that you repeat things over and over if you want to change the programming in your subconscious. This is why it is so important that you watch what you say to your children. You can't tell a little girl over and over that she is going to be like her " no-good mother" who may be a prostitute and then be surprised when in fact she turns out to be just like her. To change the negative programming in her, you must repeatedly say positive things, enough of the time, to cover up the instructions already given to her subconscious. If you have told your subconscious that you are fat, for example, it will be very hard to change it to "I'm thin". It will take constant work to change that image. This is why women who have lost lots of weight still have trouble. They still see themselves as a fat person. It doesn't matter what others say about how they look. It doesn't matter what others think. They have to reprogram their thinking about themselves until they see the new them. You can't say it one or two times and think that's going to make an impact. Built into many weight-lost programs are daily affirmation statements. You are then asked to stand in front of a mirror daily and say the positive affirmations about yourself. You must be persistent to possess your desired result. It's hard work, but it must be done to accomplish your goal. Often we begin to make positive confessions and when things don't change in a few days, we give up, stating this stuff doesn't work. Positive statements about you are important but they are only a part of the process. It's the beginning. It's the starting point. You have never won a race staying at the starting point. Remember lots of training goes into a champion in order for him to cross the finish line as the winner.

Never forget this! You are in training. There is a winner inside of you. We must run the race to obtain the prize. Remember, " I think I can, I think I can, I know I can, I will." The devil says, "No, you can't." But Jesus says, "Yes, you can."

Have you ever noticed something different, really different, about the accomplishments of great people? It seems that they had to come from further back or go through more than others do to win the race. But because they never gave up, because they persisted, they reaped the rewards of victory. That's growth, personal growth, seasoned by adversity and self-reliance. Every creature on the face of the earth, other than man, seems to pursue life every minute of every day. Plants search for water with their roots, animals seek food constantly, but man, who has a choice, puts very little effort into pursuing life in its abundance. Unfortunately, personal growth is often confused with learning. Learning comes by the exploration of skills and information outside of one's self. Personal growth comes about when the individual develops what is inside of him. The person who goes beyond what is expected finds personal growth. One must look within himself to discover who he really is. Every child, woman, and man has within himself or herself all that is needed to live a dynamic, successful, and productive life.

Some people believe that whatever card in life you have been dealt is the card you will have to play. I believe that you can control your destiny if you want to. Now that may surprise you, but it's true nevertheless. Every day you are blessed with a new beginning. You have a chance to start over again regardless of what has happened before. Each and everyday, a chance to end abusive relationships, and let go of people who put you down and hurt you. You must set a standard for yourself, not caring what others are doing, but believing that you can overcome the negatives and reach out for your future. Many times we tend to act the way we feel. Action, of course is needed for success, but you must feel success before it will happen. The human mind has the ability to imagine and visualize, and whatever we visualize, we can do. Now visualization is different from daydreaming or merely wishing. What we spend our time visualizing, or thinking about, will eventually come true. All behaviors, including yours, and mine, are learned. We make ourselves what we are. We train ourselves to do nothing rather than something and then wonder what the problem is. The problem is not in motivating yourself, but in purging your system of all the unwanted thoughts and attitudes that have been placed there through years of negative programming. Re-program your subconscious with the thoughts you want. You are designed for success. God designed you with success in mind. Your mind and body will perform what it is trained to do. The body will reflect precisely the dictates of the mind. When your behavior is not what you want, then you need to look at the thoughts being held in the mind. So when your body acts tired, lazy or indifferent, and you have an "I don't care attitude," remember, it is simply reacting to the mind's wishes. Begin today to believe you can have the success in life that is really yours by turning your beliefs into positive attitudes, which create the habits you need to change your world.

This is precisely why the Bible tells us to renew our mind with the word of God. If you don't know who you are, you need to look in the mirror and that mirror, is the word of God. It is the only thing that can give you the real truth and nothing but the truth. It describes you and sees you exactly the way God sees you, but most importantly, the way you should see yourself. However you cannot fully become the person God has destined for you to become without His awesome presence in your life. Remember that you are success waiting to be discovered. Not discovered by anyone else, discovered by you.

Pursuing self-esteem

Positive self-esteem is feeling good about you. When you feel good about you, there are things you will not tolerate in your life. You will not abuse your body by putting drugs, alcohol, or any other substance into it that would cause it harm. You will think highly of yourself and not tolerate doing things to yourself that will bring you harm. You will do whatever it takes to bring success into your life because you know that is where you are to be. Some people just let things happen to them while others make things happen. Then there are those who just watch things happen. But life does not have to be happenstance. It can be planned, and plans can be carried out. You can become the person you want to be, if you are willing to pay the price. Everything in life comes with a price. I believe we all learn that sooner or later. If you want a slim body, an education, a good job, financial freedom, etc... **the price of discipline must be paid.**

It starts with you deciding what is important to you, and with your desire to accomplish something that is important to you. Desire is where motivation begins. You need an intense, burning desire, in order to become successful in anything. There is a big difference between merely wishing for something and desiring it with an intensity that forces you to act. You must always remember your desires if they are to remain a powerful motivating force. Your motivation will carry you forth when everything that's in you, is telling you to quit.

Learn to say, "yes" to your potential. All of us have enormous potential within us waiting to be tapped. We must learn to never think in terms of limits. Someone once said that the only limitations you will ever encounter in life are those you place in your own mind, and that's true. My mother wouldn't allow me to use the words "I can't", as a child. She would always say there is no such thing as, "I can't". I remember her telling me over and over, that "the world owes you nothing, but there's a lot to be gained, if you continue to study, work hard, and obtain the finer things of life." I never forgot that and have worked hard all my life. However, I have learned that God has higher spiritual laws that were placed in the universe before time began to make my life and yours a lot easier. However, it appears I had to go through some years of training and the school of hard knocks, seasoned with adversity, to get to this higher spiritual plane.

The first thing I had to learn is that self-esteem is not a fixed trait that you are born with. It varies from one day to the next, depending upon your reactions to your environment and daily events.

As a child, raised in the south, I experienced racism from whites and blacks because of the color of my skin. Being black period meant whites discriminated against you. But being a light-complexion black also meant being discriminated against by dark-skinned blacks, as well. So I had to learn early, who I was and not allow someone else's view of me to determine who I was. I didn't understand why some of my classmates didn't like me. I was popular with a certain group, those who were on the same economic level as my family and those who felt good about themselves, but there were others who, no matter what I did, always had something negative to say. They would call me names, like "high yellow" or say that I thought I was better than they were. This would hurt my feelings because I didn't feel that way. My mother would tell me, that's what they are thinking, not you. She would help me see that everyone in life is not going to like you and that's ok, but what's important is that you like yourself. For, if you don't know who you are and don't feel good about yourself, you will always be subject to everyone else's opinion of who you are and what you should be. You will be like a little puppet on a string, being tossed to and fro, with them controlling your every emotional movement and thought.

I also learned that you couldn't please everybody. I thought if I was able to please myself and live up to the standards I had set for myself, then I was doing ok. Now you and I know, that rarely happens, especially if you are anything like myself. We place all these unrealistic rules on ourselves and suffer from low self-esteem when we don't measure up. So I had to learn that it was ok to make mistakes and that all women fall sometimes, but the great ones get back up and keep on getting back up until they finally master that thing, whatever it is, that is holding them back. I had to learn that as long as I did my best and gave it all I could, whatever it was, as unto the Lord, then, and only then, was it was ok. For as long as I felt my Father in heaven was smiling, I didn't care if you smiled or not. Now that may seem harsh, but I mean it in love. Women must get tough. Tough in pursuing who you are by looking faithfully into the word of God and seeing yourself the way He sees you. It truly is an awesome experience when you see yourself through God's eyes, the One who created and masterfully designed you. Believe me, when that happens, you will not care what these earthlings think. For the first time in your life, you will know what the scripture means that says, "If God be for you, who in the world is there to be against you". Now that is of course my translation, but you get the message.

Part of building one's self-esteem is not being dependent upon doing or achieving for one's self-identity. Being is the source of self-esteem as much as doing. If my self-identity is dependent upon getting an "A" in school, or getting a raise, or getting elected, or making a product that's best, or gaining a title, then I am jeopardizing my self-esteem. Achievement is wonderful. Attainment is rewarding. But if I need that to feel okay about myself, if I need a "success fix" every day or every week, I will gradually become malnourished emotionally.

Low self -esteem is a problem that plagues tens of millions of people who suffer daily from negative thinking and the resulting self-destructive behavior-all due to a distorted, negative view of themselves. Ranging from mild to severe, low self-esteem suppresses ambition, inhibits motivation, stifles creativity, causes chaos in relationships, and can negatively affect every aspect of a person's life.

The following is a typical example of how people with low self-esteem think: two women try out a new recipe, cooking for their respective families. Each has the same results--its not very good, but quite different reactions. Karen tells herself that the meal was barely edible, labels herself a "terrible cook," and berates herself, saying she must have done something wrong again. Sue tells herself that she didn't like that recipe, must mark it in the book so she doesn't fix it again, and is glad she didn't try it out on company. Karen, who has low self-esteem, is disgusted with herself, while Sue's feelings about herself are neutral.

Tending to personalize situations in their lives, those with low self-esteem often blame themselves when things go wrong. Processing information in this way then leads them to lose confidence and prevents them from trying new recipes, other new experiences, and limits their opportunities to find happiness and contentment in life. Those afflicted with this very common problem may avoid new challenges in life, staying in jobs where the pay and benefits are poor or destructive, or remaining in abusive relationships because they lack the self-confidence to believe they can do better.

Ironically, others may actually become over-achievers as a result of low self-esteem and do exceptionally well in their careers while their personal lives suffer. Driven by a need to receive recognition, approval and affirmation, they use achievement in the work place to prove to themselves and others that they are indeed quite adequate. As a result they may channel all of their energy into attempts to achieve in their careers, an arena in life that is more structured and thus more predictable than that of personal relationships and societal expectations. Though they suffer an inordinate amount of anxiety attaining an education and finding a job, once they do so, they strive mightily to achieve and again feel a sense of security and accomplishment in being productive. With further financial remuneration and other rewards a possibility, they remain totally devoted to, even obsessed with, climbing the ladder of success. All of this may be done in an attempt to quiet their negative inner voice that spawns self-doubt. Because recognition, respect, and accolades only temporarily assuage the self-recrimination and negative self-talk, these people seek those rewards all the more. They may become workaholics as a result, in the negative sense, neglecting all other areas of their lives.

Those with low self-esteem, who have not enjoyed early educational successes or did not receive acceptance and encouragement from significant sources outside their familial system, may spend their lives avoiding any and all new situations that pose a threat to their fear of failure. Doubting their ability to be successful, they may settle for far less than they might otherwise achieve, or worse yet, may become emotionally crippled by fear and anxiety, and/or turn to addictive behaviors in an attempt to quiet the inner voice that continues to berate them.

Another characteristic of low self-esteem is that those who suffer from it may either react as though they feel inferior or in quite the opposite manner, taking on an air of superiority, becoming defensive, argumentative, and basically obnoxious. Because of their "know it all attitude", a defense mechanism utilized to cover their feelings of inadequacy, an observer would not conclude they are reacting out of their desperate need to feel good about themselves, they have convinced themselves they are superior to those around them.

The majority of people who enter therapy have as their core issue, low self-esteem, yet it is often totally ignored or at least, inadequately addressed by many counselors and psychologists. An underlying factor in eating disorders, phobias, depression, anxiety and stress disorders, anger problems, and addictions, low self-esteem is often mentioned; but seldom dealt with - thus the symptoms and not the cause become the focus of therapy. Clients then go from therapist to therapist, feeling hopeless; eventually thinking their problem is unique and untreatable.

With proper guidance, attainment of new skills, and a realistic and rational view of themselves people can recover from low self-esteem and can lead fulfilling lives! To do this, however, they must be able to see the "big picture", cognitive work in conscious replacement of irrational thoughts, (meaning changing the way you see yourself and what you say about yourself) and positive self-statements, by itself, is inadequate. People with low self-esteem must develop an understanding of how their negative picture of self was formed and why it is inaccurate. They must become conscious of the fear and anxiety they experience, the resulting emotional turmoil, and the negative self-statements. They must also become acutely aware of how their low self-esteem is negatively impacting their lives.

Accomplishing this formidable feat of recovering from low self-esteem is possible, however, it requires time-there are no quick fixes, no shortcuts to changing the underlying attitudes and the negative view of self that are the foundation of low self-esteem. Long term therapy is, therefore, required for lasting, inner change to occur. Large numbers of both men and women are desperate to find therapists who would be able to guide them through this process of recovery from low self-esteem. Unfortunately, few therapists specialize in treating this problem and many only provide short-term therapy, leaving millions of people feeling hopeless that their lives will never change. Obviously more therapists are needed to work in this area of treatment.

As a therapist, however, I will point out some steps one can take to finding their way to high self-esteem. First, you must become more aware of your own feelings and express them in a straightforward and appropriate manner. Only you know the person, the inner child, within you. Your goal is to free the child. To attain that goal, you must be fiercely honest with yourself. You must become open to the language of feelings, your own feelings and those of others.

In doing so, you will become responsible to all aspects of your self, all dimensions of your own unique person-hood. You will end the fragmentation of the alienated self, and become a whole, integrated person. You will have the satisfaction of knowing truly who you are. In this process of growth and awareness you will find yourself becoming free of emotional baggage and unfinished business, free of obstructive clutter from the past. You will be able to like yourself without explanation or apology. You will achieve a sense of high self-worth, firmly grounded in self-trust and self-knowledge.

Take a few moments and fill out this personal evaluation. Be honest with yourself when you answer the questions. If you really look inside yourself, you will be amazed how much you can learn. Remember that the purpose of evaluation is not to prove--but to **IMPROVE!**

"If you ever hope to be somebody, be yourself; then make yourself to be the best somebody, your potential will allow."

MY HONEST DESCRIPTION OF MYSELF AS A PERSON:

*

*

*

*

" To thine ownself be true, and it follows as the night, the day; Thou canst not then be false to any man."

MY PHILOSOPHY OF LIFE MOTTO:

"Every man sets himself a certain standard. The tough part is to reach it. Without some guiding principles and decisions regarding them, we cannot know which life to live."

THESE ARE THE THINGS FOR WHICH I PERSONALLY CHOOSE TO STAND:

> *
>
> *
>
> *
>
> *

" Know thyself." - Socrates, 470-399 BC

MY GREATEST MOMENTS OF GLORY:

> *
>
> *
>
> *
>
> *

MY MOST HORRIBLE MEMORIES-EMBARRASSING MOMENTS:

> *
>
> *
>
> *
>
> *

"Memory is the file cabinet of the mind-which occasionally needs some sorting."

THE PERSON I WOULD WISH TO BE LIKE:

WHY:

QUALITIES I WOULD FOLLOW IN A LEADER:

> *
>
> *
>
> *
>
> *

"In order to learn to lead, one must first learn to follow."

MY IMPORTANT GOOD QUALITIES AND GIFTS:

> *
>
> *
>
> *
>
> *

" Every man has a particular genius- even if it's only that he can read his own handwriting better than anyone else."
MY OWN WORST SHORTCOMINGS:
    *
    *
    *
    *

What should be done about them?
Dream no small dreams for these have not the magic to stir men's souls."
MY GREATEST DREAMS:
    *
    *
    *
    *

"Be ashamed to die until you have accomplished some good for mankind."
WHAT SHOULD BE MY GREATEST CONTRIBUTIONS TO HUMANITY?
    *
    *
    *
    *

"There is no limit to the amount a human being can accomplish, if he doesn't care who gets the credit."
DAY-BY-DAY   RESOLUTIONS-ACHIEVE   SOMETHING SIGNIFICANT:
    *
    *
    *
    *

SO FAR I'VE ACCOMPLISHED THIS:
    *
    *
    *
    *

"What you are, you are now becoming."

In the next few chapters I will talk about some of the things we as women want and how we can obtain them. Each step toward self-fulfillment gives us forward momentum and raises our self-worth just a bit more. So get ready to take very good care of yourself. **You deserve it!**

In case you have some doubts about whether or not you really deserve the good things that come from self-growth and self-fulfillment, consider the following meditation on **"ME"**.

IV
"ME"

I am the only "me" I've got. There are two major parts of me. There is the inside "me" and the outside "me."

The outside me is what you see. The way I act, the image I portray, the way I look and the things I do. The outside me is very important. It is my messenger to the world and much of my outside me is what communicates with you. I value what I have done, the way I look, and what I share with you. The inside "me" knows all my feelings, my secret ideas, and my many hopes and dreams. Sometimes I let you know a little bit about the inside "me". And sometimes it's a very private part of myself.

Even though there are an enormous number of people in this world, no one is exactly like "me". I take full responsibility for "me" and the more I learn about myself, the more responsibility I am going to take. You see, my "me" is my responsibility. As I know myself more and more, I find out that I am an ok person.

I've done some good things in life because I am a good person. I have accomplished some things in my life because I am a competent person. I know some special people because I am worth knowing. I celebrate the many things I have done for myself.

I've also made some mistakes. I can learn from them. I have also known some people who did not appreciate me. I do not need those people in my life. I've wasted some precious time. I can make new choices now. As long as I can see, hear, feel, think, change, grow and behave, I have great possibilities, and I am going to grow and love and be and celebrate. I am worth it.

Author unknown

I love being me. God made me female and I love it. I enjoy being a woman and love the fact that I am a woman. I love the smell of good perfume on my body. I love getting my hair done and changing hairstyles whenever the mood hits me. I love manicures and pedicures and pampering me. I love being feminine and all that encompasses. Though, I must admit that sometimes I don't like me, I have come to like being me. More importantly, I have learned to love me, as God himself does. I am who I am, as a gift of God who made me uniquely me. Any woman with the capacity for enjoying life wants to please, wants to excite interest, wants to feel the sheer exhilaration of knowing that, as the Bible puts it so beautifully, "she is good to look upon". The desire to be physically attractive is as natural and instinctive, in men as well as women, as the desire to love and be loved. However, women today have let a lot of the pleasure go out of caring for themselves, and have become a great deal more other-directed about what constitutes beauty, not only in public figures, but also in themselves.

Members of Women's Lib say that womanly beauty is overstressed. But the desire to be attractive is as natural and timeless as human nature itself. The only vital thing is that caring for your looks should give you pleasure. I often grieve for some women who fight so energetically and angrily for male privilege and recognition that they unconsciously destroy there own qualities of femininity. On the other hand, I feel sorry for the woman who thinks so little of herself that she lays her glory down like a doormat. Especially in the delusion of false submission, which invites a man to wipe his feet on her, thinking that is the way to keep or hold onto him, but actually losing herself in the process.

If the attitude of others toward me as a woman make my performance in my position on my job or expression of my identity or calling more difficult, I will still know who I am, and receive their resistance as another exercise in forgiveness and patience. Of which, God is still teaching me.

If I were not basically secure in who I am, despite what anyone thinks of me, that decision to forgive would be difficult. But insofar as I am secure, I can meet and accept others where they are with no personal threat to my self-esteem, and no compulsive need for self-defense. Now, that may sound harsh, but it's really not. I finally began to see myself the way my Heavenly Father sees me, and I don't apologize for that. The goal of this book is to help you see yourself that way, too. Remember that self-worth is a choice, not a birthright. And it rests on one simple but all-important principle: that you begin by liking yourself, all over, and without reservations. The first step is to accept yourself fully, recognizing all the attributes you were born with.

Simply being able to make more of your looks is one of the good things of life, especially nowadays, with the wide availability of excellent beauty aids and products.

But the important thing is to enjoy it, and above all, to enjoy being you. Live a little! Your own unique physical existence is a gift to be treasured.

V
"LETTING GO"

It is impossible to raise your self-worth while living around negative people who do not see you as worthy. It is impossible for the self to thrive in a hostile atmosphere where there is little or no acknowledgement or appreciation. Feelings of worth can only flourish in a climate where individual differences are appreciated, mistakes are tolerated, sharing and communication is open, and rules and expectations are flexible. The exciting thing is that there is always hope and possibility because you can learn to make new choices that can change and renew your life.

In the past, we may have placed energy and resources in friendships that did not flourish. It's time to let go and move on. Clinging to false hopes keeps us from our own growth. In every risk, there is bound to be some loss, something that has to go in order to be able to move ahead. Becoming comfortable with loss is a part of growing.

Now that statement may be very hard for some of us to take, but nevertheless, it's very true.

Some people stay in relationships because they seem secure. Even though we know that the relationship is conflicting with security; in fact, it's the very opposite. Others take and stay in dead-end jobs because they fear new responsibilities. Still others gravitate to groups because they dread being alone. There's an undercurrent of fear that pulses through them incessantly, a message from the scared inner child, which states, "I am unlovable, I had better settle for what I have, I'd better not take any chances."

Yet the paradox is that until we give up all that feels secure, we can never really trust the friend, mate, or job that offers us something different. Personal security that is based on truth, does not come from without, it comes from within. When we are really secure, we must place our total trust in our God and in our self.

If we reject deliberate risk-taking for self-growth, we will inevitably remain trapped in our situation, or we end up taking a risk unprepared. Either way, we have placed limits on our personal growth and have cut ourselves off from action in the service of high self-worth.

Primarily, what we are talking about here is the risk to be your self. It seems such a simple thing. We've heard it from childhood: "just be your self". Simple, indeed, on the surface, yet no other risk is so fearful and fraught with anxiety.

People who are afraid of being themselves, cheat themselves out of finding out what life is all about. To go through life pretending to be something you are not or feel what you really don't, is not being real. It's being dishonest and phony. Real prestige and self-worth is not built upon pretense. If you do not risk changing when the time is right, you will probably be forced to change when you are least prepared for it, and the changes may not be healthy ones.

The risk we must take to attain a more honest life are always more difficult at the beginning, but the life we are creating by taking the risk is limitless and starts looking like a world full of possibilities.

Exactly one year after my divorce, a co-worker introduced me to her friend at a dinner party. She had told me weeks earlier that I needed to meet this guy. At the time, I was "gun-shy" and was afraid to take the risk. The day of the dinner party I had planned to call her and make some excuse as to why I couldn't come and not show. She must have sensed it and called me before I had the chance to call her. She insisted that I come, even if only for a few minutes. Little did I know that this meeting was to teach me a very powerful lesson and change my life?

Before I tell you about him however, I must tell you how God prepared me to meet him, even though I didn't know it at the time. Awakening one night, God began to speak to me. I grabbed a pen and began to write as He spoke. He said, "Women need to let go of so many things that have held them in bondage for far too many years. This is the hour, God said, that I am raising them up to be what I've called them to be. But first, they must put aside every weight that has held them captive by the enemy, and they must know that I have never consulted their past to decide their future and their destiny."

One of the first things, we must let go of is fear. Fear of being what God wants you to be; fear of feelings that have robbed you of your destiny: fear of thinking you're not worthy or not good enough: fear of stepping out of your comfort zone into the realm of faith and truly trusting God to be that person He has called you to be.

Fear of just relying upon God to be your total supply instead of feeling that you need to help God out by having a "sugar daddy" on the side or by playing the lottery or going to the casino to pay your bills.

Fear of thinking God will not really feed you, clothe you, provide for you, and deliver you.

Fear that He will not break those chains that kept you locked away from your destiny.

God is saying to you now, that if you will heed to His voice in this hour, spend time with Him and sup with Him, then will you hear from Heaven and be the woman that He has created you to be.

The second thing we need to let go of is past hurts and pains. We must let it go.

Some of us are holding onto pains and hurts that happened years ago. You say, but you don't know what they did to me---you don't know what happened? And I say to you, "It no longer matters." A hard truth to meet head on is that some relationships needed to end and some still do. Have the good sense to walk away and LET IT GO!

You must release the past and let go of the regrets about what happened back then. Finding fault or blaming yourself and others keeps you stuck in the past and away from the inner healing that needs to take place so you can march into your future.

We serve a right now God and if you let it go and let God, he will heal the hurts and heal the pain. What are they worth? Are they worth keeping you from receiving all that God has for you or all that He has created you to be?

By holding onto that pain, you are kept in bondage. It keeps you locked up with chains of resentment and hate. It keeps you locked up with feelings that eat away at your very soul. Let it go.

It keeps you in fear of being hurt again, afraid to trust and afraid to love. And soon, before you know it, you are right back into fear. Many of us have been afraid for so long, that we don't label our feelings fear. We're so use to feeling upset and anxious that it feels normal, and peace and serenity feels uncomfortable.

God says in 2nd Timothy 1:7, "for God has not given us the spirit of fear, but He has given us the spirit of power, love and a calm, well-balanced and disciplined mind".

Many of us were oppressed and victimized as children and as adults we may continue to keep ourselves oppressed. Some of us don't recognize that caretaking and not setting boundaries will leave us feeling oppressed.

Some of us don't know that we hold the key to our own freedom. That key is honoring us, and taking care of ourselves.

It's time we say what we mean, and mean what we say.

We must stop waiting for others to give us what we need and take responsibility for ourselves. When we learn to do that, then the gates to freedom will swing wide open. All we have to do is walk through.

Repeat after me...

"Today, I will understand that I hold the key to my freedom. I will stop participating in my oppression and victimization. I will take responsibility for myself, and let others do as they may."

50

peccadillo

The third thing we need to let go of is negativity. Some people are carriers of negativity. They are storehouses of pent-up anger and volatile emotions. Some remain trapped in the victim role and act in ways that further their victimization. Others are still caught in the cycle of addictive or compulsive patterns.

Negative energy can have a powerful pull on us, especially, if we're struggling to maintain positive energy and balance. It may seem that others who expel negative energy would like to pull us into the darkness with them.

We can't change other people. It doesn't help others for us to get off balance. We don't lead others into light by stepping into the darkness with them. It always amazes me when a good wife will allow her husband who is deep in peccadillo, convince her that in order for their marriage to work, she must begin to do all the sinful things he is doing. One wife told me she even allowed other women into their bedroom because her husband was bored with their love-making and he said this was a way to improve their marriage.

When you begin to do anything that violates your values, principles and character, then it is wrong and you shouldn't do it. So what if he likes it, what about you?

Repeat after me…

"Today God, help me to know that I don't have to allow myself to be pulled into negativity, even around those I love. Help me set boundaries. Help me know its okay to care for myself."

The next thing we need to let go of is guilt. Feeling good about us is a choice. So is feeling guilty. When guilt is legitimate, it acts as a warning light, a signal that we're off course. But then its purpose is finished.

Wallowing in guilt allows others to control us. It makes us feel not good enough. It prevents us from setting boundaries and taking other healthy action to care for ourselves.

Even if we've done something that violates a value, extended guilt does not solve the problem: it prolongs the problem. So make an amend. Change the behavior. Then **LET GUILT GO!**

The last thing we need to let go of are those loved ones or people in our lives that are not willing to change.

Several years ago, I read this story which clearly illustrates what I mean. "Picture for me a bridge. On one side of the bridge, it is cold and dark. We stood there with others in the cold and darkness, doubled over in pain. Some of us developed an eating disorder to cope with the pain. Some drank. Some used other drugs.

Some of us lost control of our sexual behavior. Some of us obsessively focused on addicted people's pain to distract us from our own pain. Many of us did both. We developed an addicted behavior and distracted ourselves by focussing on other addicted people. We did not know there was a bridge. We thought we were trapped on the cliff.

Then some of us got lucky. Our eyes opened, by the grace of God, because it was time. We saw the bridge. People told us what was on the other side; warmth, light, and healing from our pain. We could barely glimpse or imagine this, but we decided to start the trek across the bridge anyway.

We tried to convince the people around us on the cliff that there was a bridge to a better place, but they would not listen. They could not believe. They were not ready for the journey.

We decided to go alone, because we believed and because people on the other side were cheering us onward. The closer we got to the other side, the more we could see, and feel that what we had been promised was real. There was light, warmth, healing, and love. The other side was a better place.

But now, there is a bridge between those and us on the other side. Sometimes, we may be tempted to go back and drag them over with us, but it cannot be done. No one can be dragged or forced across the bridge. Each person must go at his or her own choice, when the time is right. Some will come; some will stay on the other side. The choice is not ours.

We can love them. We can wave to them. We can holler back and forth. We can cheer them on, as others have cheered and encouraged us. But we cannot make them come over with us.

If our time has come to cross the bridge, or if we have already crossed and are standing in the light and warmth, we do not have to feel guilty. It is where we are meant to be. We do not have to go back to the dark cliff because another's time has not yet come.

The best thing we can do is stay in the light, because it reassures others that there is better place. And if others ever do decide to cross the bridge, we will be there to cheer them on."

Yes, God never consults your past to decide your future. We have all had problems, but don't ever let that stop you. If you study the lives of great people, they all had one thing in common; they all dealt with problems. For example, look at Fanny Crosby, who was blind but wrote many of the gospels hymns we sing today; or Harriet Tubman, who led over one thousand slaves to freedom and was wanted dead or alive for doing so. But in her death, was hailed and praised by presidents and heads of state; or Martin Luther King who had the struggle of the Black man in his heart and in his being, who dreamed that his children and our children would be known by the content of their character, instead of the color of their skin.

Our situations and circumstances may look pretty bleak, but when we take time to look at the accomplishments of others that have persevered, we can take heart and have courage.

Your life is only over if you think that it is. You can learn to "glory" in your infirmities and build a bridge out of them to find God's purpose for the rest of your life.

Think about....

Bill Wilson, who was a "hopeless alcoholic," founding Alcoholics Anonymous, which has brought sobriety to millions; or John Milton doing his greatest literary work after he became blind at forty; or Core ten Boom becoming a world inspiration with her books and films. She had been released from a Nazi concentration camp in her fifties, after she had lost her entire family; or Ludwig van Beethoven creating his greatest symphonies after he started going deaf. Vowed the music master: "I will seize life by the throat."

You need not draw inspiration from just the famous. Draw from the example of LaRue Moss who was told by her father when she left for college, "Honey, if you're going to reach out for the stars, first you have to put out your hand."

LaRue aspired to be an educator. First, she fell in love. Six weeks after the wedding she broke her back in an auto accident. It was three years before she could walk again. She almost died in childbirth and was bedridden for a year.

Finally, she went back to school and completed her bachelor's degree in elementary education--sixteen years after her father had taken her to the bus station to leave for college. She attended school while operating a lawn mowing business to help support her family.

She enrolled in a master's degree program while continuing to mow lawns. She was studying for her doctorate at Vanderbilt University in Nashville when a hit-and-run driver struck her down. Despite chest injuries and a bruised heart, she managed to stay in graduate school.

A dull backache continued and intensified. The doctor said she might be paralyzed within twenty-four hours if she didn't have surgery. Leaving her incomplete dissertation, she was whisked into the operating room.

She awoke in a sunlit yellow room to see the beaming faces of her family. "I thought I had died and gone to heaven," she said. Then, looking at her sister she asked, "Hey, did you bring my dissertation back from the waiting room?"

Sixteen months later, this brave woman who kept "reaching for the stars" received her doctorate in education.

You must remember that without resistance there is no progress. Without the resistance of air, the plane cannot fly. Without gravity, we cannot walk.

Some of us want a testimony or a victory celebration without having to go through any hardships or any resistance. Remember, without a fight, there can be no victory.

If we don't confront our mistakes, they mock our miracles. If we don't deal with our failures, they will make fun of our success.

If you never had a problem, you will never know God as a Deliverer, as a Savior, and as a Healer.

So now, do you see why it's time somebody told you?

I needed to let go of the image I had of men. Thinking all men were like my ex-husband was keeping me in bondage and not allowing me to meet the man whom would eventually be the husband God intended for me to have in the first place.

Knowing what you need as a woman is great, but knowing what you want in a man is fantastic. Be sure you know what qualities you seek in a man and then be just as sure the man you allow into your life possess these qualities. I often have women who come in for therapy write down everything they want in a relationship and everything they want in a man. I have them list the qualities they look for and expect in a man. Qualities like character, integrity, honesty, values, etc... I then advise them to continue adding and deleting from the list for several weeks until they narrow it down to an exact image. I have them do this for two reasons: one, so they will get a clear picture of what they want, and will know him whenever he is presented to her. And, along with that, so they will not accept anything less than that. Many women allow "blockers" in their life. All that "blockers" do is waste your time. "Blockers" are what I call men who are just there in your life, blocking your good from coming to you. You both know that the relationship is never going anywhere, but he's just there, a warm body taking up space in your life. When Mr. Right does come along, he can't get to you because Mr. Blocker is in the way. Expect the best for yourself by expecting what you want as a woman. Don't be afraid to aim high and stretch yourself. If your man doesn't challenge you, he may not be the one. Learn to practice aiming high, rather than lowering your expectations, to make them more achievable or realistic. Yet, very unrealistic expectations can be a form of self-sabotage. Don't expect that your knight in shining armor will find you in a day or even a week---it may take longer---just remember to stick to your list of requirements for your dreamboat, so you will be able to recognize him when he appears.

Your wish list will probably have enough on it to fill several pages. That's ok. Keep working on it until you narrow it down to what matters most to you and what excites you. It's important that you do this without any help from your girlfriends. What matters to you may not matter to them, so do this alone. As you set your priorities and write down the things you like in a man, also write down the things that most men have said they like in you, then compare the two. You might find there is room for improvement in you.

Don't be afraid to accept the fact that you have flaws. Be a woman about it and accept your shortcomings by working to improve yourself. Most importantly, don't expect the man of your dreams to be flawless, because no one is perfect, not even you.

As you expect and demand the qualities you want in a man, remember not to cheat yourself. Your happy life starts with you, and as a woman, your happiness is your number one priority.

Because I finally learned what I wanted and needed, it placed me in a position for my **Boaz** to enter my life, and believe me, I am able to clearly recognize him when he appears. Oh, who is Boaz? Well, let me tell you about him.

Do you remember the beautiful story of Ruth in the Old Testament? Well, a woman named Naomi and her husband left Bethlehem with their two sons. They traveled to Moab, which means "a cursed place." There, outside of the will of God, Naomi's husband and two sons died. The two sons had married Moabite girls, and one of them, Ruth, chose to return to Bethlehem with Naomi. Ruth also chose Naomi's God. So Ruth was a believer; she was redeemed, but she was to experience the fuller meaning of redemption during her stay in Bethlehem!

Ruth gleaned barley in the field of a very rich man named Boaz. He was a relative of Ruth's dead husband, and Mosaic Law made it the duty of the next of kin to marry the widow and raise children in the dead man's name. Boaz desired to marry Ruth; but in order to marry her, he first had to prove his family ties to her dead husband. Boaz's brother was actually the next of kin. Boaz married Ruth out of desire more than duty. He asked his brother to give up his right to marry Ruth. Then he had to buy back the land that used to belong to her husband, and, finally, be willing to raise his children under Ruth's dead husband's name. This was called the law of the Kinsman redeemer.

The Hebrew word for redeemer is "gaal," and it is translated eighteen times as redeemer, fourteen times as kinsman, and six times as avenger.

Jesus is all of these things to you and me. He is our kinsman; He emptied Himself of His divinity and came down to earth clothed in humanity. In order to be your relative and understand you, Jesus was tempted in all ways and paid the price for your sin: Jesus became your kinsman redeemer.

It's easy for us to believe that God will redeem us when we're innocent victims of oppression, but when the bondage is our own fault, we sometimes think God is going to sit back and watch us squirm to get free. No, He won't! Look what happened to Israel: after God set them free from bondage to Pharaoh, they eventually turned their backs on God and were taken into Assyrian and Babylonian captivity.

God could have said, "Tough luck. You're guilty. Get yourself out of this one! He didn't. (Isaiah 62:12)

The Jews had blown it---they had forsaken the Lord---and were led away captive. God still considered them "the redeemed." After they had repented, God brought them back into the Promised Land. God will bless you, too, if you'll repent and turn back to Him. Always remember: you are "the redeemed" of the Lord. God has nothing but good planned in your future, but until you allow Him to deal with the negative experiences that have shaped you, they will be a "ball and chain" that will keep you from living in total victory. Believe me, there is a place in God where a man or woman can live in victorious circumstances at all times. Many people say that can't happen until you get to heaven, but thank God, his Word says differently.

VI
"DON'T CHEAT YOURSELF"

Remember, I said a friend introduced me to a friend of hers at a dinner party. Actually, he was her assistant pastor, who in the previous year, had gone through a terrible divorce. She thought the world of this man and felt very strongly that we should meet. Everyone loved and respected him, and felt he was the victim in an unfaithful marriage. He was like no man I had ever met. He was handsome, intelligent, honest, confident, successful, had integrity, and most important, a Christian. He actually lived the life he preached about. We had so much in common that we instantly became good friends. He was extremely patient and allowed me to be myself. We could talk for hours and never get tired. He would listen, asked questions, and didn't feel as if he had to know everything. He appeared confident in himself and was not afraid to be vulnerable. For a verbal person as myself, with a type A personality, this was heaven. It was as if I had known him all my life. He became my best friend and I fell in love with him. I thought he was the man of my dreams; the one who would be my best friend as well as my spouse; the one that I could talk to about everything; the one who would be the spiritual head of our home; the one whose values were similar to mine; the one who had integrity that I longed for in a man, and the one who knew what commitment meant and valued it. We communicated so well that it shocked us both.

My daughters loved and respected him. I remember one of them asking me one day, what I like the most about him. I thought for a moment and said to her, "he celebrates me." He told me once that I was his dream and he was clearly my dream. To be able to spend the rest of your life with your dream is awesome and to think that God had put you together is even better. Remember, I said that I was about to learn the most powerful lesson of my life. You see when I divorced my ex-husband; I went through a year of inner healing along with my daughters. I was bitter and didn't trust men. I thought all men were like my ex-husband, told lies and were unfaithful. God showed me what His man was like, a true Christian man. I totally respect this man and have learned a great deal from him.

I have always had a problem with patience. Because of my busy schedule, I hate to waste time. I had trained myself to think fast and make decisions quickly. I assess the situation and then make a decision. This guy was just the opposite. He was a thinker. He would look at a situation a million times, pray over it and then wait before he decided what to do. It's not that either way is right or wrong, we were different and we learned how to compliment each other with our differences. However, at first, I must admit, he nearly drove me crazy. I am a workaholic and although we both had demanding schedules, he took much better care of himself by getting the proper rest he deserved. I am still learning, but doing better at that very precious and valuable lesson.

In fact, studies show that women today are seeking more and more ways to relax. I have found for me that solitude works best. Because I am a therapist and spend much of my time listening, talking, and helping people solve their problems, the best way for me to relax is to spend time alone. Solitude has rich possibilities for inner peace and personal development. Setting aside time to listen to yourself allows you the time to see the world around you more clearly. Even though good conversation is stimulating, remaining quiet for hours at a time also have wonderful benefits and allows you to gain spiritual insight.

I have found that effectively incorporating solitude into your life helps you to relish and value life. By observing silent times when you don't speak, don't answer the telephone, don't read the newspaper, watch television, or listen to the radio, you can listen to yourself instead, especially if your spirit is born-again and tuned into God. In fact, some of the best times to solve problems are during silent times.

Ella Patterson in her book, "Will the Real Women...Please Stand Up!" stated that, silence should be programmed into the life of every woman. "Women tend to appreciate the input from their surroundings by drawing on their personal energy. Traditions of silence are ancient and full of spiritual enlightenment. Silence is known as the "holy uselessness," a cleansing of interfering vision. Even though the dictionary describes silence as passive, the absence of speech or noise, many philosophers consider it active and complex."

Psychiatrist Anthony Storer, the author of, "Solitude: A Return to the Self," explains how a woman wrote him to tell how she escaped to her bedroom each afternoon, not because she needed to sleep but because so much of her time was spent being alert to the needs of others, that she needed to be alone.

"Silence creates a sanctuary of self-observation. Many people distrust silence because society discourages it; therefore it is feared. Since quietness is seen as rejection or fear, it is not easy to recognize it as the inner voice of strength. Some people call it arrogance, while others see it as a form of sadness. Silence has been smothered in today's busy and noisy world of information. Reviving the values of silence is now being done at retreats and religious centers so that the mind can be nourished by tranquillity. Retreats often provide spiritual renewal. Many times silence releases the power to express yourself. Women are seeking contemplation in our society, and they are finding out that they don't have to leave home to obtain its benefits."

"Silence can be discovered in your everyday life. Creating an environment to succeed with silent commitment is necessary to capture its true benefits. Here are some basic guidelines to follow:

1. Have the person or people with whom you live actively cooperate. Cooperation is crucial to your growth in silence.

Silence can sometimes feel like rejection to your loved ones, so explain why silent times are so important to you. Using these times as curtains to enclose yourself instead of a door to shut out loved ones will help create the support needed from your family.

2. Share your silence. Being quiet together can add new life to your relationship. It's okay to smile, to touch and to look in to each other's eyes from time to time with nonverbal communication.

3. Bring your children into your circle of silence. Encourage them to bring silent times into their own lives. It helps them to value the ability to concentrate as well as make graceful exits from arguments. It enables them to release stress by learning to calm themselves.

4. Schedule silent times. Set aside time in your day for being completely silent. You can choose the time of the day as well as the amount of time you'll use. You're making time for you so you can make the rules.

5. Explain silent times. It's your decision whether or not you explain your personal solitude. People are going to form their own opinions regardless of the true reason, so why not be unavailable during these times. After all, isn't that the purpose of silent times?

6. Ways to spend time during solitude:
      **Enjoy a long quiet ride alone in your car.
      **Take a walk in the early morning day.
      ** Take a walk in the quiet evening dusk.
      ** Take a quiet walk along the beach.
      ** Take a silent bike ride with your lover.
      ** Encourage a quiet hike.
   **Sit on a hilltop and recapture the essence of nature.

**Enclose yourself in your favorite room in your home and lavish solitude upon yourself.

You may want to do something different each time you reward yourself with silence. You may choose to quietly cook, clean, garden, write poems or short stories. A quiet place offers creativity. Doing nothing at all is also nice for nourishing your soul.

7. Make use of the tools available to you. Use your answering machine to intercept your telephone calls while integrating silent times at home. Silence is new to many women, so exploration is different. Capturing the world of silence is an intimate relationship with oneself."

Remember the business of taking care of you is in the hands of you more than anyone else is. You've got the power to be the best that you can be if you start with a little positive personal adjustment. Many of us take our greatest abilities so much for granted that we don't even know we have them. To bring your personal assets into focus, take inventory. On a piece of paper, list your good points and don't be modest. Divide another piece of paper into two columns. On the left, list everything special or unusual you've done---starting with your childhood, if you can remember. On the right, note the traits that these reflect. Now, compare these columns with your first sheet. You're almost certain to spot assets you didn't know you had. Last but not least, an ideal goal to attract the man of your dreams includes a plan to strengthen your personal weaknesses. Strengthening your personal weaknesses can be beneficial to meeting the man of your dreams. It will not only improve you as a person, but it will also help to improve your standards and thereby help you to reach higher goals-like finding that lucky someone who has been waiting for you all his life.

Don't underestimate your ability to improve yourself no matter how many times you've already tried. If you really want to change yourself for the better, begin now. Don't put it off another day. Do it for you! By mapping out a plan and being flexible as well as resourceful, your dream will become a reality. Remember to shine, even if the sun doesn't. Stop looking at where you have been and start looking at where you can be. **You cannot be what you are not, but you can become what you are not.**

Tomorrow you will be what the sum of today's thoughts leads you to be. Let's say you have indicated some need to change and let's say you now know what areas you need to change. You are now ready to accept the fact that you can change and that you are already changing. You must also accept the responsibility for which you will become, and go for it. Now you must also learn that change is good and in order to learn that, we must look at change and how to develop the right attitude toward change.

- **People can change and will change,** if and when they want to, have the resources for change, and be highly motivated to change.

- **People tend** to change when they have meaningfully participated in the decisions to change.

- **People tend** to support change which they personally help design; they tend to resist change when they do not help design it.

- **People tend** to change when they are convinced that the rewards for change exceed THE PAIN OF CHANGE.

- **People tend** to change when they see others changing, particularly when the direction of change is supported by valued persons.

- **People tend** to change more readily in an environment free from threat and judgment.

- **People tend** to change more readily when they personally have, or can   acquire the competencies, knowledge, and skills required by the change.

- **People tend** to resist change to the degree that they feel it is imposed upon them. A sense of free choice is essential for people to be free to change.

Accept the fact that you can change. Get rid of all that you do not want. Decide what you do want. Then look at the rewards of change. Then finally, put action to it. Remember you must learn that **change is good.**

   If your life is ever going to change for the better, you'll have to take chances. You'll have to get out of your rut, meet new people, explore new ideas and move along unfamiliar pathways. In a way the risks of self-growth involve going into the unknown, into an unfamiliar land where the language is different and customs are different and you have to learn your way around.

   When we are ready to grow, we are ready to give up the way we usually see ourselves, which is risky. After all, our old reliable self---no matter how inadequate or unworthy-that's the only sense of self we know. What happens if we lose ourselves and nothing takes place? What happens if we obliterate the very essence of our being---ourselves?

   As we take risks, as we move in the direction of growth, we start taking new "pictures" of ourselves, if only in our imagination. We decide we are ready to give up false beliefs, compromises, relationships, poor investments (job, money, energy, volunteer commitments, and so on), superficial attachments and self-destructive habits. Relinquishing these ingrained aspects of our lives can be difficult, but it's absolutely necessary for growth to take place.

   Change for me was very good. Yes, it was risky, but it was good and oh my, how I grew as a result of it. By changing, God has allowed me now to be in a position to meet my Boaz. A very important lesson I learned from that previous relationship was that although it looks like love, many times its not love. When God sends you someone, he will have everything on that list I told you about earlier, not just most of the things on the list. The devil always has a counterfeit. And in my situation, even though this man was a good man, a Christian man, and always treated me with the utmost respect, he still was not the one for me. I will always care for him because he showed me what a Godly man looked like and it changed my image of men. I had been so naïve before. My ex-husband had been my high school boyfriend and I married him. He was the only man I knew. The years I knew this man, I felt safe and secure, which I never felt in my marriage, and it taught me another lesson about myself; my need to feel safe and secure.

It is so important to take your time, not be in a hurry and remember that God loves you so very much. When you ask him to bring your mate to you, he will. You don't have to look for him. The man that finds a wife finds a good thing. He will find you. Just be ready to be found. And never cheat yourself.

VII
"THE VIRTUOUS WOMAN"

One day, as I was having a discussion with my friend, I asked him, just how did he see me? Now whenever you would ask him something, you must be prepared to here what he had to say, because he would always tell you the truth, regardless of whether it hurts your feelings or not. He would not try to hurt your feelings, but he would tell you the truth. He just didn't lie. So I prepared myself to hear what he would say and what he really thought. He looked at me for a brief moment and said as a matter of fact, "I think you are a **virtuous woman**". My heart skipped a beat. He was always complimenting me, but that was by far the nicest compliment he had ever said, because I knew that he knew what that meant, and I also knew that if he didn't think it, he would have never said it.

In speaking of the virtuous woman, Proverbs 31:10-31, Solomon, in verse 10 writes,

"A capable, intelligent and virtuous woman, who is he who can find her? She is far more precious than jewels, and her value is far above rubies or pearls,"

This statement is confirmed in I Corinthians 11:7, where it says, "...but woman is (the expression of) man's glory (majesty, pre-eminence)." She is the glory of her man, because she is the extension of his purpose. She is a reflection of his successes, (and if she is a good wife, she hides or covers his failures with her love). This constitutes her being the glory of HER man. The virtuous woman is our example of excellence, the ideal model after which we should pattern our lives. She is a woman after God's own heart and her value is far above rubies or pearls. A ruby is a precious stone used to create beautiful jewelry. Its price ranges from moderate to expensive. Proverbs 31 references this stone, declaring that it cannot compare in value to a woman who is virtuous. In fact, the worth of a virtuous woman is esteemed higher than the costliest of rubies.

In the eleventh verse of Proverbs 31, it goes on, *"The hearth of her husband trusts confidently in her and relies on and believes in her safely, so that he has no lack of honest gain or need of dishonest spoil." The NIV states it this way, "Her husband has full confidence in her and lacks nothing of value."*

They are united together in spirit, soul and body. They have agreement for their purposes in life. She is not belittling him and has not wounded his male ego (initiative). She is content with what they have, whether they are abased or abound, working with him so he trusts her. It is hard for a man to trust his wife if there isn't a mutual purpose, in their lives and agreement on how it is to be fulfilled. If she is continuously trying to make something out of him that he isn't and has no desire to be, he won't be able to believe in her, and won't rely on her for fear or failure, feeling degraded, etc. The virtuous woman is honorable, truthful, intelligent, confident, capable and supportive. She is mentally, spiritually and physically fit. Her primary focus is the well-being of her household, and she doesn't overextend herself by getting involved in ventures that may cause her family to suffer.

Verse twelve: *"She will comfort, encourage and do him only good as long as there Is life within her."*

Verse thirteen: *"She seeks out the wool and flax and works with willing hands to develop it."*

Her attitude is that of submission, allowing him to make decisions and take responsibilities. I don't mean that she doesn't make some decisions. Her life is just not a cop-out, in other words. There are some women who have been made to believe that **any** place of submission to their husband is a place where they have no voice and no responsibilities. This is far from being true, and if we watch to see exactly what this virtuous woman is doing we're going to see that she has a lot of decisions to make, and she takes responsibility.

Verse fourteen and fifteen: *"She is like the merchant ships loaded with food stuffs, she brings her household's food from a far (country). She rises while yet it is night and gets spiritual food for her household and assigns her maids their tasks."*

There is much to be done. She has maids to help but has to know how to plan their duties, in order for them to be of help to her. She's an organized woman. She is an astute businesswoman and a good steward of her resources. Also, she has made time for her personal devotions with the Lord and sought after "spiritual food" for her household. To me this is the intercession she makes each day in her spiritual language, for her family, overthrowing and destroying strongholds of the enemy (II Corinthians 10:4).

Verse sixteen: *"She considers a new field before she buys or accepts it –expanding prudently (and not courting neglect of her present duties by assuming others).*

With her savings (of time and strength) she plants fruitful vines in her vineyard."

She's no dummy! She is a businesswoman for the sake of her household. She is a worker!

And she is not lazy. She is not sitting around doing wishful thinking, waiting for her ship to come in. No, she aggressively goes and gets her ship and manages it well.

Verse seventeen: *"She girds herself with strength (spiritual, mental and physical fitness for her God-given tasks) and makes her arms strong and firm."*

She accepts the fact that she is a triune person and has responsibilities to herself in the spirit, soul, and body.

As we read these next verses, meditate on them and see what the Holy Spirit is saying to you.

Verse eighteen to twenty-seven: *"She tastes and sees that her gain from work (with and for God) is good: her lamp goes not out, but it burns on continually through the night (of trouble, privation or sorrow, warning away fear, doubt, and distrust). She lays her hands to the spindle, and her hands hold the distaff.*

"She opens her hand to the poor: yea, she reaches out with filled hands to the needy (whether in body, mind or spirit).

"She fears not the snow for her family, for all her household are doubly clothed in scarlet.

"She makes herself coverlets, cushions, and rugs of tapestry. Her clothing is of linen, pure and white and fine, and of purple (such as that of which the clothing the priests and the hallowed cloth of the temple are made).

"Her husband is known in the city gates, when he sits among the elders of the land.

"She makes fine linen garments and leads others to buy them: she delivers to the merchants girdles (or sashes that free one for service)

"Strength and dignity are her clothing and her position is strong and secure.

She rejoices over the future-the later day or time to come (knowing that she and her family is in readiness for it).

"She opens her mouth with skilled and godly wisdom, and in her tongue is the law of kindness-giving counsel and instruction.

She looks well to how things go in her household, and the bread of idleness (gossip, discontent and self pity) she will not eat."

We see that this virtuous woman has the positive attributes of strength and dignity, knowing the role she is to fulfill in her home and feeling strong and secure in this position. Her mind transmits wisdom and kindness so that through her mouth come words of good counsel and instruction, refusing to fellowship with thoughts and words of gossip, discontent and self pity which could destroy her and her household.

Now we can look at the effect all of these virtues have had on those around her---look at this positive response!

Verse twenty-eight to thirty-one: *"Her children rise up and call her blessed (happy, fortunate and to be envied); and her husband boasts of and praises her, saying, 'many daughters have done virtuously, nobly and well (with the strength of character that is steadfast in goodness) but you excel them all."*

"Charm and grace are deceptive, and beauty is vain (because it is not lasting), but a woman, who reverently and worshipfully fears the Lord, she shall be praised!

"Give her of the fruit of her hands, and let her own works praise her in the gates of the city!"

Isn't that beautiful? Praise God! To hear our children and our husband declare that non excels her, is such a wonderful reward. To know that he thinks you "excel them all" is the highest of compliments, and when he comes to you and says, "You're the GREATEST! I'm so glad you're mine"---don't you know our woman heart leaps for joy to know we have fulfilled our role in his eyes, and that he believes you are truly a gift from God. To have our children say, "mom, you are the best, I'm so glad you're my mother." To have your children look to you as their role model, instead of some of the ones they are choosing today. Now, that's a wonderful reward!

Becoming a virtuous woman requires a commitment to becoming whole through the word of God. Wholeness is a state of being complete, nothing lacking, missing or broken. It cannot be accomplished overnight, but it can be attained. The characteristics of a virtuous woman are influenced and modeled by the word of God. She has learned to put God first place in her life. She has learned, through submission to His word, how to live free from stress and walk in His perfect will. His word becomes the final authority in her life. She knows that by putting Him first in her life, He will provide all the things that she needs, and her household will rise up and call her BLESSED!

VIII
"INNER BEAUTY"

To successfully have the outward appearance of radiance, vibrancy and happiness, we must also have inner peace. As Christians we have learned by the Word and experience that peace is acquired by development in the soul and spirit areas. When our character, which is made up of our attitudes, emotions, will and intellect begins falling in line with the Word of God, our spirit comes to be at peace and rest with God, others and ourselves.

When there is peace on the inside, there will be an outward manifestation of it, and we will be at rest in all areas of our life. The object then, is to have the spirit controlling the body and soul. I can't emphasize that enough. Before we are born again, the soul and the body are in control. The spirit is quenched and hindered inside of us. Unless you were born again when you were very, very small, and had proper teaching, knowing positive responses and who you are in Christ Jesus, your spirit probably hasn't fully developed.

Let me help you, we are a three part being. We are spirit, we have a soul, which is made up of our mind, will, and emotions, and we live in this physical body. When we are born-again, by accepting Jesus Christ as our Lord and Savior, our spirit man is born-again. We still have this same body that wants to do all the things it has been use to doing. This is why the Word of God tells us that our mind must now be renewed with the Word so that the change on the inside can now be reflective on the outside.

"Whose adorning let it not be that outward adorning of plaiting the hair, and of wearing of gold, or of putting on of apparel; But let it be the HIDDEN MAN OF THE HEART, in that which is not corruptible, which is in the sight of God of great price." 1 Peter 3:3,4 KJV

Kenneth Hagin, who was a great man of God, explains this passage the best I have ever read, he says, "no one knows what you look like. They may think they do. But they don't. You—the real you—are a hidden man. You are a spirit, you have a soul, and you live in a body (1 Thess. 5:23). What people see is the house you live in." He states he has heard ministers' quote two-thirds of 1 Peter 3:3 and say women shouldn't fix their hair and shouldn't wear gold. But if that's what Peter meant, then women shouldn't wear clothes. For if he told them no to plait their hair, and not to wear gold, then he also told them not to put on apparel. Apparel is clothing. No, Peter is really saying, probably because women are more prone to do this, "Don't spend all your time on your hair, on your clothes, and on the outward man. But see to it first of all that the **hidden man of the heart**—that's the spiritual man, the real man, the inward man—is adorned with a meek and a quiet spirit."

So, if you are unhappy, and you do not have inner peace, chances are that:

* You cannot accept yourself.
* You are having trouble accepting others.
* Your happiness is dependent on other people and the way they treat you (e.g. the way your husband treats you, the way your children or your friends treat you)
*You depend on surrounding circumstances for happiness, such as more money, social status, physical beauty, new clothes, sharp car, beautiful house, etc.
* You think that if you had less pressure and less responsibility that you could be happier.

All of these things mean that you are looking to the flesh and to the five senses for comfort and happiness.

Joy and inner peace come only through Christ Jesus. In order to have a character change; we must have the right relationship with God. Having that right relationship, and learning to see ourselves the way God sees us, we can learn to accept others and ourselves just as we are, faults and all. That is a big accomplishment. This does not mean that we will not seek improvement or expect others to improve, but just that we can be more accepting of ourselves and others.

In finding inner peace, we find joy, which is a fruit of the Spirit. Joy brings strength to our character. It also brings right attitudes and emotions. In Nehemiah 8:10 it says,

"...And be not grieved and depressed for the joy of the Lord is our strength, and stronghold."

And my, how many times does a wife and mother need additional strength? You'll find that inner strength comes by the Spirit, and the fruit of the Spirit. Strength is the fruit of joy. The joy of the Lord is our strength! So, knowing joy, spiritual joy, because He is Lord of our lives, and knowing all of our needs are met in Him, brings us happiness and inner peace.

This means knowing our spiritual place in Christ Jesus and our position in high places with Him:

"But God, who is rich in mercy for His great love, wherewith He loved us, even when we were dead in sin and hath quicken us together with Christ by grace ye saved) and hath raised us up together and made us to sit together in heavenly places in Christ Jesus, that in the ages to come, He might show the exceeding riches of His grace in His kindness toward us through Christ Jesus" (Ephesians 2:4-7) KJV

When you finally realize down in your spirit that you are sitting with Jesus by the throne of God, what greater joy could you possibly have? All the power, all the strength, all the health, all the provisions for life are yours because you are in Christ Jesus. This gives you inner happiness. You have to know this. You have to know it down in your spirit, and the only way you are going to get it into your spirit is by the Word of God being "computerized" into you, and coming out as faith, power, and positive responses in your life.

Joy does not know anything about happiness. Happiness is a fleshly thing. Joy comes from the spirit. Joy is a spiritual force. It could care less what the physical senses say, or what the circumstances are. When you feel down and out, or even if at night when your husband says, "Honey…Baby", and you feel like "Let's go to sleep!" the joy of the Lord can manifest in your spirit to come through that body and give you the strength you need to minister to your husband in body ministry. That's just a plain old practical situation, and it happens in most houses every night. So let's apply it where we can use it. An automatic response to inner peace then, is a smile and a pleasant countenance. Remember again, that this glowing, fresh, contented appearance is appealing to your husband.

Do you want him to pay attention to you? Then be appealing to him. You have to make your body appealing to your husband. You may have wondered why there are so many temptations to our men. Outside of our homes, other women are paying attention to our men, and they are making themselves appealing. This should challenge you. You have to maintain appeal even in your own house. It doesn't mean that every day you have to go around like a raving beauty, but there does have to be some semblance of beauty--a happy, fresh, vibrant appearance that is appealing to him, letting the "Son shine" out.

Think about it. There will not be one person that is going to want to look at a woman if she looks sad, depressed, dejected and disheveled, and say, "I'd like to be with you," or "I want what you have!" As we allow the Holy Spirit to work through our spirit to manifest this joy and peace in our body, on our face, in our eyes and in everything about us, we will glorify God in our bodies and others who don't have it will want what we have. That inner peace that only the Son of God can give. Let's look again at 1st Peter 3: 3-5.

"Let not yours be the (merely) external adorning with (elaborate) interweaving and knotting of the hair, the wearing of jewelry, or changes of clothes: but let it be the inward adorning and beauty of the hidden person of the heart, with the incorruptible and unfading charm of a gentle and peaceful spirit, which (is not anxious or wrought up, but) is very precious in the sight of God.

For it was thus that the pious women of old who hoped in God were (accustomed) to beautify themselves, and were submissive to they're husbands-adapting to them as themselves secondary and dependent upon them."

In years of doing marriage counseling, I hear women over and over point fingers at their husbands as the reason they are unhappy. When I began to work with them to help them see themselves the way God sees them and to let them know they have the goods to bring their man back to the place he should be in their home, revelation takes place. Most women don't realize that they are anointed to minister to their husbands in a way that no other woman can. As she learns this, she learns she can have heaven on earth and in her bedroom, too. A male client recently told me (as I was trying to help his wife soften up and understand that men and women are different), "Please tell her again Dr. Williams, I don't want a man in my bedroom, I want my wife to be feminine and allow me to be the man." Sometimes women are so cold and hard, and they wonder why their spouse is turned off to them.

I find so much of the time that I have to teach them that they are different and as a result of their differences, they see things differently. Man and woman were designed by God from the beginning to be distinctly individual, free to make choices, yet created to be vitally one with each other.

"He created them male and female, and He blessed them, and named them Man in the day when they were created. (Gen. 5:2)

Each person, male or female was created in the image of God, male and female, with both male and female attributes. Man is designed to experience and act primarily out of the masculine role of his being, and yearns for the woman to meet him. In their one-fleshness she will express that part of him, which he cannot. Woman is designed to experience and act primarily from a uniquely feminine base, though she has masculine qualities within her. Her husband is to unite with her in such a way as to fulfill and express easily that masculine part of her, which she cannot.

Many Christian wives want to preach to their spouses, but not live the life they preach about. The fruit of kindness is not preaching the Word at your unsaved husband, nor is it telling him all his faults, but it is the ACT OF SHOWING him you care. It will bring him to repentance. That is why I Peter 3:1-2 says,

" *In like manner you married women, be submissive to your own husbands-subordinate yourselves as being secondary to and dependent on them, and adapt yourselves to them. So that even if any do not obey the Word (of God), they may be won over not by discussion but by the (godly) lives of their wives, when they observe the pure and modest way in which you conduct yourselves together with your reverence (for your husband. That is, you are to feel for all that reverence includes)-to respect, defer to, revere him; (revere means) to honor, esteem (appreciate, prize), and (in the human sense) adore him; (and adore means) to admire, praise, be devoted to, deeply love and enjoy (your husband).* "

The wife's behavior, love and fellowship, is body-soul ministry to him. If the wife does all we have discussed in the soul and body area, the Holy Spirit is free to work through her with the fruits her man can see. It will bring him to repentance, and right on into the Kingdom of God. He doesn't have a chance! Glory to God!

One of the best examples I have heard of in this area was Smith Wigglesworth's wife. He was by trade a plumber who was in a backslidden condition for a number of years who later became a famous minister of the Gospel. He went "all out" for God, evangelizing, casting out demons, laying hands on the sick and seeing them recover. It has even been reported that three people were raised from the dead in his ministry. His wife had lived with him for many years, simply being a GOOD and godly wife. She gave him a happy home.

The part of the story I would like to emphasize here, begins on a day when she had taken good care of him, had given him his dinner, and put everything in order. She had paid a lot of attention to him, (if you know what I mean), and, having done all this, she told him that she wanted to leave to go to church. He said, "No.

You spend too much time at church. If you go to church, I will lock the doors and you won't be able to get back inside." She told him, "Well, Smith, I have to go to church! I love the Lord and He said for us not to forsake the assembling of ourselves together." She needed the fellowship of other believers. So, she went to church, having fulfilled her body-soul ministry to him. She loved him. Smith was being cantankerous, that was all. She went on to church, came home, and sure enough, he had locked every door. She didn't have a key so she couldn't get in. She took her coat, pulled it up over her, and sitting at the back door, stayed there all night.

In the morning she could hear him getting up. Not too much later, he came out, opened the door and looked at her. She jumped up, and said, "Good morning, Smith! What would you like for breakfast?" Now, that's an attitude! Thank God, she was married to Smith, because I couldn't have done it, especially where I was mentally in my marriage. However, Praise God, that I have grown and have continued to learn, and now know, that there is tremendous power in submission.

That's what you call being humble and submissive. Look at the results. God took that humility and submission, and exalted her. Because of the kindness and love she showed to him, body-soul ministering to him, he came to the Lord and was filled with the Holy Spirit. He became one of the greatest faith-men known in our time. It has been reported that people were actually raised from the dead during his ministry.

She gave us a good example, didn't she? Submissiveness is something that you give. It cannot be demanded. It is an attitude of the heart. You have to decide to be submissive.

We have given you natural principles and spiritual laws as to why you should submit, but submission is your decision. We must also clarify that Godly submission does not mean being a doormat for your man. **NO MAN WILL ULTIMATELY RESPECT YOU IF HE IS ALLOWED TO WALK ON YOU.** Here, balance comes up again.

Remember that there is a difference between being submissive and being a doormat. In counseling I have heard many women say things like "My husband didn't want me to come to this counseling appointment (or to church) because he wanted me to do so and so with him." Well, some of this won't hurt anything, but if you make a habit of putting your fellowship with man before your fellowship with God, you will quickly find yourself in a backslidden condition.

A Christian wife must hold true to her commitment to the Lord. If it has to be at the cost of losing her unbelieving husband because he can no longer subject himself to her love for God, then the Word says she is free. I Corinthians 7:15, says:

"But if the unbelieving partner (actually) leaves, let him do so; in such (cases the remaining) brother or sister is not morally bound. But God has called us to peace."

Please notice that the believing wife is to body-soul minister to her husband (read all of Chapter 7 of 1st Corinthians) doing all she can to keep her marriage intact.

Remember, if you are in the right---God sides with you, but be sure, you are in the right.

It was important for me to know that I had done everything I could do to save my marriage to my first husband. So when it did end in divorce, I had no regrets in that area. I didn't have to question or second-guess myself. Of course I felt badly, because no one likes to fail at anything and this represented a failure for me. But I knew I had done all I knew to do. I also knew that I was ok with my Heavenly Father, and that was the only thing that mattered at the time. I knew if my conscious was clear, I could go on with my life and allow the inner healing that needed to take place, take place. It's been twelve years since the divorce and my ex still calls and begs me to come back. I think he has no peace in that arena because he didn't do all that it took to save the marriage. He did just the opposite, all he could, to tear it apart and just like the song says, "you don't miss your water until your well runs dry."

Leo Buscaglia outlines the strength of a good relationship in his book "Loving Each Other":

The very measure of a good relationship is in how much it encourages optimal intellectual, emotional and spiritual growth. So, if a relationship becomes destructive, endangers our human dignity, prevents us from growing, continually depresses and demoralizes us-and we have done everything we can to prevent its failure-then, unless we are masochists and enjoy misery, we must eventually terminate it. We are not for everyone and everyone is not for us. The question is, "If we cannot be with another, can we at least not hurt them? Can we, at least, find a way to co-exist?"

I agree with that statement one hundred percent. Sometimes couples stay together for the sake of the children, and end up doing so much emotional damage to themselves and the children that it would take years for a therapist to fix, if he or she could.

When abuse is present in a relationship, you must exercise some common wisdom and get out. There is no honor or glory in staying in that type of relationship. Some people end up eventually dead. Remember God has called us to peace. Believe me, it would be better for the children to live in two separate homes that are stable, than live in one home that is quite dysfunctional and abusive.

IX
"PRINCIPLES OF THE UNIVERSE"

Each of us knows and understands something about the Law of gravity. We cannot see it, touch it, smell it, or hear it, but each time we stand up or lie down we experience the effect of this law. It doesn't matter whether or not we believe in this law or not, it still controls our behavior. When we arise each morning, our feet fall to the floor. We are not capable of walking on the ceiling, and our belief in the law has no bearing on our reaction to this law of the universe. Life is composed of many laws and principles. In this chapter we will take a closer look at the principles of the universe and how they are available for everyone to use to help them become the greatest person that they can be. These principles will in fact help you or they will work against you. It matters not if you believe in them or not. If you do not understand them, they are still going to affect your life. They are there and they work.

I was introduced to these principles many years ago and I am still learning how to successfully apply them to my life. To have a better tomorrow, we must start with a better today. By starting today at learning the secrets of the universe and the laws that control your future, you will have the tools necessary to change your life for good. For, just like the law of gravity, these laws are always at work. Learn to use them and how to benefit from them. They are:

Principles of the Universe
   * Principle of Choice
   * Principle of Organization
   * Principle of Meaning

* Principle of Multiplication
* Principle of Intensity
* Principle of Trust
* Principle of Measurement
* Principle of Exclusion
* Principle of Need
* Principle of Truth.

Together these 10 principles will work to help you accomplish anything in life that you can perceive in your mind. Notice that the first letter of each one, when placed together, they spell **COMMITMENT**.

The first principle is the **Principle of Choice:** (There are no "have to's in life, only want to's). Despite what most people think, we do not "have" to do anything in life. By not doing anything, your life will be void of meaning and the things God has for you will not take place. Every single day, you have a choice to do something, but you don't <u>have</u> <u>to</u> do, one thing. If you do anything, it is because **you want to. You do the choosing.** Many may make the choice because their spouse or children want them to, or you may feel pressured into it by someone else, but nevertheless, only you can chose to do it. Even if it's only to please someone else, it's still your choice. No matter what you do, you choose to do it. It's always your choice. Positively or negatively your attitude will always affect the outcome of your decision. If you feel "I have to do this," and you really don't want to do it, you will not do it well and the outcome will produce negative results. But when you feel "I chose to do this," your attitude will produce a positive outcome, because it is something you want to do. As you learn to control your thinking regarding any situation, not be led by others, and remember the choice is always yours, you will discover the power that lies within your soul to be the captain of your own ship. . Remember, the Bible clearly states, "a double-minded man can't receive anything of the Lord." Control your thoughts and your will, by making your own decisions. Stop blaming others for the choices you make. It doesn't matter what others may have done to you; you still have the choice on how you will respond to them. No one can take you to that place called "there," but you. You know what I mean. When your spouse, friend, or just anyone rubs you the wrong way or pushes that wrong button; and you are "there". You are in a fit of rage as if you can't control yourself. You must remember then, more than ever that the choice is always yours. You can go "there" or remain in control of self.

The second principle is the **Principle of Organization:** (Get started and do it now)

You made the choice to accomplish something with your life. It doesn't matter what goal you have set, now it is up to you to make things happen. Begin by organizing and developing a plan of action. Approach your goal or activities you have planned with a positive attitude. Be specific with your plan of action. Learn to do the things that need to be done, when they need to be done. Organize yourself in terms of priorities. These include organizing your life, your time, your skills and effort. Don't leave out any details. It may include organizing your desk, your room, your materials, cutting off the television, getting off the phone, etc. But organize everything you need to accomplish the task so that you will complete your goal. Because I do so many things, I must organize everything, or I simply cannot function. My children tease me because I can tell you what shoe is in every box in my closet. Now, you may not think that is organization, but I possess over a hundred pair of shoes, and I know which one goes in what box. Things are so organized in my home that I use to tell my children if anyone had been at my house when I was not home. When my girls were teens, they thought I had them watched or something. We laugh about it today, but I was so organized, that I could tell when I walked into my living room if anything was out of place. I have a specific place for everything in any room in my house and it just stands out when it's not where I placed it or not like I placed it. All three of my daughters are excellent housekeepers today because of those organizational skills they learned at home.

The third principle is the **Principle of Meaning:** (Develop a deep, burning desire; be passionate about your dream). The outcome of anything you do is directly in proportion to the amount of desire with which you begin. You have decided what you want to do, you are organized, and now you must develop the desire. When you want to do something, all that remains is to get started. The burning desire will motivate you to persist until you accomplish your goal. Picture in your mind what you want, write it down, and think about it every morning and night. The desire that results will be all the motivation you will ever need. Then fan the fires of desire by reading your goals daily. The constant repetition will drive you to accomplish the task. Now focus the goal in your mind and hold it there. The power of visualization will enable you to achieve success. Place yourself in the picture with what you want to accomplish. Actually see yourself doing what you desire, and unleash your creativity. No matter what you want, build a burning desire for its accomplishment with your thought processes. Give it time, take appropriate action and it will be yours.

The fourth principle is the **Principle of Multiplication:** (Take what you have and increase it tenfold.) Multiply your chances of success by using more of your potential. God has given you the potential for greatness. You are capable of accomplishing anything you can visualize yourself doing. The things you can visualize doing with your life reveal what is possible. You are probably using about 15% of your potential, which unfortunately is the norm for most people. Take the limits off your potential by thinking big. Start earlier, work smarter and do more than is expected of you to increase your potential. I saw a sign some years ago as I entered a school building that read, "Are you working harder or smarter?" You cannot expect to win the race of life if you do not use the power that is yours. That power that God has given to each of us to accomplish the purpose for which we are called. Therefore, multiply your successes by increasing your potential. The potential is there. It is your choice. Will you use it or lose it?

Principle number five is the **Principle of Intensity:** (Put everything you have into everything you do.) You will find success comes only to those who put forth the necessary effort. If you can develop the habit of doing more than is expected of you, you will soon develop the habits that lead to success. Learn to put everything you have into everything you do and be willing to sign your name to it. Let people know you are the one responsible for the outcome of everything you begin. Put your best into life to get the best back.

Number six is the **Principle of Trust:** (Trust is belief and belief is faith). Belief is trusting in the fact that what you want to happen will happen. You cannot memorize a list of principles and expect something good to happen. You must put your trust in them and believe with all your heart that they will work. You must believe it will happen before it happens. If you must see it first in the natural, then faith or trust is of no value. People go through life wishing for something and saying that "if" it happens or "if" I get the job, then I will be happy. Do not say "if", say "when." Act as if it has already happened. Trust in yourself and in what God can do through you. *"Trust in the Lord with all your heart and lean not on your own understanding; in all your ways acknowledge him, and he will make your paths straight."* Proverbs 3:5,6 NIV

Ben Carson, M.D. Director of Pediatric Neurosurgery, John Hopkins University, wrote in his autobiography that "who could have believed that the worst student in Higgins Elementary School fifth grade would one day become a world-famous brain surgeon; that a poor ghetto kid would learn to perform operations too risky for some of the most highly trained surgeons to attempt; that the kid who got zero out of thirty on his math quizzes would regularly snatch the lives of tiny children from the edge of death?"

He stated that his mother believed and would tell him many times that, "If you ask the Lord for something and believe he will do it, then it'll happen." His life is living proof that it is true.

Principle number seven is the **Principle of Measurement:** (Evaluation shows progress, progress brings excitement.) Seeing progress will help reinforce belief. If you will constantly evaluate your progress, you will soon become very excited about the possibility of achieving your goal. If you can see what you want is going to really happen, the excitement generated inside will keep you moving forward and nothing will stop you. Learn to evaluate daily and to measure your progress. Be persistent. Keep at it. Remember the Little Engine, "I think I can, I think I can," and before you know it, little by little, your dream has become a reality.

Principle number eight is the **Principle of Exclusion:** (Get rid of what you do not want and make room for what you do want.) Be careful of what you put into your mind for it will affect your behavior. For years you have been programming your mind. The thoughts that you have been putting in are now used to solve problems, make decisions, communicate, and do everything you do. Most of your programming has been negative in nature. Remember that psychiatrists tell us that by the time we are sixteen, we are already programmed with over 140,000 negative thoughts about ourselves compared to about 100 positive thoughts about ourselves.

To have the best life you can live, you must erase all negative thoughts in order to make room for the positive thoughts. You must learn how to feed your faith and your doubts will starve to death. You need to control what goes into your subconscious because it is limited in its ability to perform by the raw material you give it. This is why Romans 12:2 states, "Do not conform any longer to the pattern of this world, but be transformed by the renewing of your mind. Then you will be able to test and approve what God's will is -- his good, pleasing and perfect will." ...NIV

The ninth principle is the **Principle of Need:** (People do things because of wants and needs.) Here is the basis of all self-motivation. Our motives are our reasons for doing anything. We are all motivated by those things, which we need or want or perceive to need or want. We are always trying to satisfy certain needs. Young girls may spend hours in front of the mirror trying to look their best because of the need to be liked, accepted or loved. We all have a need to belong to something that really counts for us. All of us have that need, including you, and you will work to fill that need. Get to know yourself, and to know what your wants and needs are. The need to be okay is the greatest need we have. We will do most anything for people who help us feel wanted. All human beings have the same basic needs:

*To belong, to be meaningfully involved in something which really counts.

*To feel success in genuine achievement which he regards as his own thing.

*To feel compassion, freedom, and discovery.

*To be able to use his life to make a difference in his own world.

*To live comfortably in the face of constant anxiety

*To cope with threats against his identity-both real and imagined.

*To feel genuine control over his own destiny, to create his own future.

*To be responsible for his own behavior, to know the consequences of it, and to face them in total acceptance.

*To own a self-concept which is real, relevant, appropriate and respected.

*To have a number of chances to become a better person than he is right now and the freedom to want to.

*To develop a capacity for sharing strong feelings of affection with at least one other person.

*To be open to change and personal growth. To become an agent of constructive change in the world and to value the outcome, the process, and the traditions.

*To have an ideology he can value and share.

*To have a chance to learn as much as he can, as well as he can, as fast as he can about what is true in the universe.

*To have a will to try and a reason to want to.

Learn to evaluate your needs, deciding if they are true needs or just wants. Then determine to accomplish your needs and learn the secret of contentment. *"I know what it is to be in need, and I know what it is to have plenty. I have learned the secret of being content in any and every situation, whether well fed or hungry, whether living in plenty or in want. I can do everything through him who gives me strength."* (Philippians 4:12,13 NIV)

Principle number ten is the **Principle of Truth:** (What I perceive to be true is more important to me than what is really true.) Perception is how you view your world. It is how you see yourself. The way you view yourself is the single most important factor in the quality of your life. Your perception of yourself is very important. Other people can influence your thoughts, but it is what you think of yourself that matters. It's the basis of self-esteem. Self-esteem is how we "see" ourselves; it influences much of what we do, including what we become. What you perceive is true is true to you. If you think you can or if you think you can't, you are right!

Get to know the person who is truth and you will get to know you. No one knows a thing better than the creator of it. God knows you. Allow him to tell you who you are, not the fashion magazines or the movies or the rock stars, or the romance novels that so many women get caught up in, wanting that to be their reality. Jesus said, *"I am the way, the truth and the life. No one comes to the Father except through me."* (John 14:6). It is only with a relationship with the Father that we can expect to know our purpose for being here. How can a man know the meaning of a thing unless he asks the creator of it?

In this world, there are two types of truth, received truth and revealed truth. It is one thing to receive a truth, and another to have it revealed in you. When revelation takes place, it becomes your reality. When that happens, you will base your life on it and change will come. For example, just knowing the word of God, received truth, will not benefit you. The only way to benefit from the word of God or from **the truth**, as God refers to himself, is to make it a standard for living, because it and of itself, just knowing the truth, will not effect change. You must make it your reality, which will change your life.

Let me give you another illustration from a human point of view. Abraham Lincoln freed the slaves, right. But even though they were free, only a small number left the plantations, and took advantage of their freedom, compared to the thousands that were set free. Many remained in bondage because the truth received had not been truth revealed. Just knowing a factual truth will not effect change. In their case, it had not yet become their reality, in which to base their life on, so they remained in bondage. *"If you know the truth, the truth will make you free…"* John 8:32, NIV **Remember**, bondage cuts off the voice of God, which is where the devil wants you. But God will give you the opportunity to hear His voice again and to experience true liberty.

These principles will work for you if you will use them on a daily basis. Try them and see what happens. If you use them and believe in them and expect them to work, I guarantee you they will produce positive results in your life.

I would like to challenge you to move from where you are to where you really want to be. Begin to apply all the principles of the universe to everything you do. READ, STUDY, GROW, AND BECOME all that God has destined you to be. Write a plan for your life, and then invest time in becoming the person you want to be. There is no magic wand. No one can do it for you. If you will do the things we have talked about earlier and apply the ten principles, your life will take on new meaning and you will never be the same.

Remember, we all have dreams of what we want to achieve during our lifetime, but few "endure to the end" to see their God-given dreams become realities. To achieve our dreams we must first set a long-range goal and objective. Without specific goals, nothing significant can happen.

After we have set our objective, we must think about the specific steps we can take to reach this goal. As we take each step, we are making a commitment to press on. The only thing that helps us at this stage is perseverance. Perseverance makes it possible for us to believe that we can accomplish what we've set out to do.

Perseverance is not an easy quality, yet it's not a quality for a select few. Most of the time, it involves an amount of courage that we would never believe we could have. It's a unique combination of patience plus endurance. It's what makes life worthwhile in spite of adversity, and quite often, it involves a quality of letting go and letting God keep us at it, funneling his power through us to keep us from quitting. I must confess that there are days I want to crawl into the corner and never come out, but God, who is always by my side and who has promised never to leave me, keeps me steady on my path.

Plus, I know full well that I don't have a corner on the pain market. I simply share these things to help us realize more fully that we all face tough times, emotionally and physically, as we feel discouraged, and think about giving up. At one time or another, giving up is exactly what we're all tempted to do in any undertaking or any crises that stretches us, because such tough situations open us up to risk and failure.

There are times even, when we are forced to do a laborious task-and then do it all over again. But if we follow it through to the end, the results can be better than we expected. The following story about author Thomas Carlyle (1795-1881) is an excellent example of what I mean.

Thomas Carlyle had finished writing his tremendous manuscript, History of the French Revolution (1837). He gave it to his neighbor, John Stuart Mill, to read. Several days later, Mill came to Carlyle's home pale and nervous to report to Carlyle that his maid had used the manuscript to start a fire!

Carlyle was in a frenzy for days. Two years of labor lost. He could never muster the energy to write again. A task that large was overwhelming the first time. The thought of having to write the whole thing over was almost paralyzing.

One day, as Carlyle was walking the streets, he saw a stonemason building a long, high wall. He stood watching for a long time before he was suddenly impressed with the fact that the wall was being built one brick at a time! He took inspiration from that experience and decided, "I'll just write one page today, and then one page tomorrow. One page at a time, that's all I'll think about."

He started small and slow. The task was tedious, but he stayed with it and went on to finish the work. The end result was better than the first time!

Don't let bad memories or unfortunate incidents move in and dominate you. You won't get far by looking in the rear-view mirror-- you must look ahead! Perseverance enables you to live in such ways that you can make good things happen.

Don't make excuses. Anyone can make an excuse, but a real woman will take responsibility for her actions and for herself. You can't just say it; you have to do something. If you want a job, you have to look for one. If you want a spouse, you have to make yourself attractive. God provided manna, but if the Israelites hadn't gone out and picked it up, they would have starved. In Matthew 9:2-7, Jesus said to the man with palsy, "Rise, take up your bed and walk." The attempt to rise was difficult and painful, but he had to make the effort. Had he not tried to rise, he would never have been healed--but he did try and by doing so, discovered his healing. You have to make an effort too--it may be hard, it may be uncomfortable, and you may have to keep on trying, but when you make the effort, you will discover that God has answered your faith prayer, and already given you the power to succeed.

Has God dropped an idea, a dream, and a goal into your heart? Well, it's harvest time! It's time to take those "impossible" labels off your dreams and discover that, with God, they are possible.

Your dream defines your reason for existing and gives you the key to your future. A "dream" is defined as a fond hope; a strong aspiration or desire; an anticipation of a positive expectation. You see, your dream not only gives you a hope and an expectation for your future, but acting on it brings you the fulfillment you long for.

Unfortunately, some people never acknowledge their dreams and never find the purpose for their being. But Jesus not only places within you His dream for your life, but also the power of the Holy Spirit, which will enable you to fulfill it.

X
"DARE TO BE DIFFERENT"

There are many things that shape you and prepare you for life's journey. A person does not become a man or a woman simply because of his or her chronological and physiological development. Becoming a man or a woman is an educational process that can best be learned by emulating men and women, who have respect for themselves, and allowing them to become positive role models for you.

Growing up in the segregated south, I experienced many things, but probably the most painful thing, segregation and discrimination, turned out to be the most positive, in that it allowed me to experience difficulties which forced me to be strong and develop the strength and character I have today.

Someone once said, "If life gives you lemons, if you are smart, you'll learn how to make lemonade." That of course is my translation, but I decided long ago, during that experience, that I was not going to allow anyone's remarks or opinions, to make me feel bad about myself, nor would I allow anyone else to define me. I would define me. In doing that, I learned the secret to developing a positive self-image. That it doesn't matter what others believe or think about you, the only thing that really matters is what you think of yourself.

Henry Ford said, "Whether you think you can or whether you think you can't, you're right." If you can imagine it, you can achieve it. If you can dream it, you can become it.

The identity of a person is very important. It helps you to know who you are and who you are not. It also helps you to acknowledge your heritage and your culture. For, in knowing both of those factors can you draw on the strength and wisdom of your ancestors to enable you to be a strong and viable person today.

Remember, I said earlier that you should emulate positive role models that respect themselves and others. Well, allow me to introduce you to some of my role models, my heroes, those individuals who dared me to be different and who challenged me to be all I could be.

First, were my parents, who taught me to believe in myself and that I could accomplish anything in life that I wanted to accomplish as long as I was willing to pay the price through hard work, faith, skill, and perseverance. Mother would not allow us to use the words "I can't." She would say, "There is no such word, any time a person uses the words "I can't", that person is trapped." Then she would quote, Charles Dubois, who said, "Be able at any moment to sacrifice what you are, for what you could become."

I would like to challenge you today with some of my role models and see if they will challenge you as well.

I challenge you today to-----

Dare to be different, when all around you seek conformity like Bessie Coleman, who broke racial and sexual barriers in her short aviation career. Bessie grew up in poverty, in the Texas cotton fields. Bessie had a drive to better herself and became an avid reader. By using the traveling library that came through two or three times a year, Bessie managed to finish high school (not a small achievement in those days). After graduating from high school, she joined her brother in Chicago, where she enrolled in beauty school and later got a job as a manicurist. She went one day to see an air show and became fascinated with airplanes. She read everything she could find on the subject of flying. Her dream was to learn how to fly an airplane. She applied to flight schools in the U.S. but was denied because she was an African American and because she was a woman. Following the advice of a friend, the

92

ambitious Coleman saved her money and later traveled to Europe, where she took flying lessons from French and German aviators. In 1921, she became the first American woman to earn an international pilot's license. She was determined to get ahead, and show the way to others, handicapped by what she believed were the evils of racism, poverty, and ignorance. Bessie returned to America yearning to open a flight school for blacks. She began touring with air shows and astounded audiences with her daring maneuvers. She believed "the air is the only place free from prejudices." It was at great personal sacrifice that she pursued her dreams. Her life was a quest for equality in the air. For that she wrote, "Whatever happens, there shall be no regrets." She persevered against many obstacles to accomplish her dream. Bessie died in 1926, at the age of thirty, during a test flight in Jacksonville, Florida after her aircraft malfunctioned and crashed. She died young, but not before she had really lived. She pursued her goal, fulfilled her dream, and is remembered by young and old as a woman who dared to be different.

Dare to seek new and greater challenges when all around you are procrastinating like Shirley Chisholm, who was the first Black woman elected to Congress and the first woman to run for President of the United States. Although she did not win the nomination in 1972, her effort encouraged other minorities to run for higher political office.

Dare to encounter obstacles when all around you avoid conflict like Jesse Owens who entered the 1936 Olympics in Berlin, Germany. At the time Adolph Hitler was the leader of Germany. Hitler believed and told the world that the Germans were the "master race." Jesse was bombarded with threats on his life. One threat stated that if he even showed up to run, he would be killed. Jesse not only showed up, he ran and became the first athlete, black or white, to win four gold medals at a single Olympic game.

Dare to have faith when all around you, are doubting like Dr. Daniel Hale Williams, who was the first person, black or white, to perform open heart surgery. He also started Provident

Hospital, the first hospital that was operated entirely by blacks. A man, James Cornish, was stabbed in the chest and taken to Provident Hospital. It appeared he would die, but Dr. Williams did the only thing that seemed sensible to him at the time. Dr. Williams opened his chest, repaired the heart, and Mr. Cornish lived for another 20 years.

Dare to remain strong when all around you are weakening like Thurgood Marshall who was the first black to be named a Supreme Court Justice of the United States. His decisions concerning the rights of all citizens have brought great changes to our American way of life. He was the attorney in the famous Brown vs. Board of Education of Topeka, Kansas case. Through his efforts, in 1954, the Supreme Court made segregated public schools illegal. The hardship of having to wait on tables to get through law school did not stop him. He became one of the best legal minds in this country.

Dare to continue when all around you are quitting like the "Little Rock Nine" who in 1957, when I was 10 years old and watching this on television, decided to test the law passed in 1954 that outlawed segregated public schools. Although, the law had passed, schools still remained segregated. The NAACP selected seventeen black teenagers to enroll in Central High School. However eight withdrew out of fear, and only nine were brave enough to try to enter the school. The students became known as the "Little Rock Nine." The governor even sent the National Guard to keep the blacks students out. The President of the United States had to order the United States Army to protect the blacks students. The "Little Rock Nine" finally entered Central High School and made history.

I challenge you today to---

Dare to see possibilities when all around you see only the impossible like Harriet Tubman who was the conductor for a very special "train." She never ran her train off the track nor ever lost a single passenger. Many called her the "Moses of her people." Harriet Tubman led over one thousand slaves to freedom. In 1884, Harriet married John Tubman, a free man. Several years later, her slave master died. Fearing that her new master would sell her out of state, Harriet Tubman decided to determine her own fate. She would escape. Her husband laughed at her plan and refused to go with her. However, two of her brothers liked the plan and decided to run away with her. Armed with a rifle, they set out. Midway through the journey, her frightened brothers turned back, but Harriet wanted freedom badly, and alone she made her way to freedom and safety in Philadelphia.

She wasn't satisfied that she was free; she longed to help her people gain freedom. She made nineteen trips back to the south and rescued over three hundred slaves. They had little to eat and lived in constant fear, but pointing her rifle, the fearless conductor would often tell those who were afraid to continue, "You'll be free or you will die." At one time, there was a $40,000 reward for Harriet's capture. She said her greatest triumph came when she helped her aging parents escape. In 1863, she led the Union Army on a raid that freed 750 slaves. In 1913, in her nineties Harriet Tubman died, and was mourned by blacks and whites alike. She was given a full military funeral. Many officials spoke of her strong qualities and her contributions to her fellow man. In 1978, a Harriet Tubman postage stamp was issued in her honor.

I challenge you today to---

Dare to dream even if no one dreams with you like Abraham Lincoln whose mother died when he was a small child. As a young man, he ran for the legislature of his state, but he was defeated. He entered business, but a worthless partner put him into bankruptcy. He fell passionately in love with a girl, but she died. He served one term in Congress, but was defeated for re-election. He tried for an appointment to the United States Land Office, but failed to get it. He tried to be a lyceum lecturer, but he failed in that also. He ran for the United States Senate, but was defeated. He ran for vice-president of the United States, but was defeated. He kept on dreaming. Friends tried to tell him to forget it, but he kept on dreaming. Others thought he was crazy, but he kept on dreaming. And then one day, he ran for the President of the United States of America, and won.

And finally, I challenge you today to---

Dare to lead, when all around you are looking for a leader like Rosa Parks who on a cold evening in December 1955 in a simple act of protest gave way to a new era of the civil rights movement. It was on that day that Rosa Parks, weary from her job as a seamstress, was ordered to give up her seat to a white passenger. Her refusal to move to the back of the bus demonstrated not only her courage but also her defiance of society's injustices. Her subsequent arrest sparked a 381-day bus boycott and has earned her recognition as the "mother of the civil rights movement."

In 1980, at the 25th anniversary celebration of the bus boycott, Parks received the Martin Luther King, Jr., Nonviolent Peace Prize, the first woman recipient of the award. In 1984 she was given the Eleanor Roosevelt Woman of Courage Award at a ceremony in New York.

Three years later she received the E. Joseph Prize of the Jewish Institute of Religion for being the "mother of the modern freedom movements." On June 15, 1999, Parks was given the greatest honor awarded by Congress, the Congressional Gold Medal. Rosa Parks stands out as a symbol of courage and the continuing fight to make democracy work in the United States.

One of the great joys of my life was in meeting and talking to this very humble, but gentle giant among men and women who dared to be different.

Too many of us let the little things in life defeat us. Many outstanding figures in history have had to overcome obstacles before they became successful, and then perhaps that is part of what made them so great. Struggle is placed in our life many times, to make us strong and give us the strength we need to face the giants, so we can overcome.

These have been some of my role models growing up. There are many, many others, but reading the stories of these courageous men and women not only helped me to discover the principles that I used to guide my life, but it taught me about my black heritage, my American heritage and about America itself. I feel it is crucial that we know the heroes and heroines of our history and to also realize that the price African Americans paid in our struggle for equality in America was dear. In addition, we must also understand that we have gotten as far as we have partly because America's democratic system and ideals made it possible.

In April of 1999 while on a five-city tour of Italy, I began to appreciate America's democratic system and ideals more and more. We are so blessed in this country, even to the point of being spoiled really, when compared to the rest of the world. Yes, we are still struggling with racism and prejudice, but the great men and women that I mentioned above are a tribute to the spirit of our democratic ideals and the system in which they and we have flourished. And that makes their stories special, and worth knowing.

Each one of these great Americans challenged me in many different ways. They spoke out from the past to strengthen me on my journey, to not only deal with the difficulties that each and everyday brings, but to encourage me to face the uncertainties in my future with dignity and grace.

As some of you begin your journey, and to others, who are well on their road of self- discovery, I offer this advice, **"Don't hate the struggle."** Embrace the struggle. You are that diamond in the rough. As you take the challenges, apply the principles, and discover who you really are, I guarantee you will come forth as a shining sparkling diamond. The future is not a spectator's sport. It's not what will happen; it's what you will do about it, that counts. And since God is still the same today as He was yesterday,

97

we can always expect Him to take us on to victory, each and every time, as we put our total trust in Him. **Enjoy the journey!**

WORDS OF WISDOM

There comes a time,
we know not when,
that marks
the destiny of men (and women). --Joseph Alexander

For I know the plans I have for you,"
declares the Lord,
"plans to prosper you
and not to harm you,
plans to give you hope and a future.

Then you will call upon me
and come and pray to me,
and I will listen to you.

You will seek me and find me
when you seek me with all your heart."

---Jeremiah 29:11-13 (NIV)

REFERENCES

Chapter II
The Double Diamond Principle, by Mike Murdock, Wisdom International, Inc., Dallas, Texas, 1990
Family Violence Is No Longer Just A Family Matter...Family Violence Is Everybodys
Business!, Anne L. Ganley, Ph.D., the Family Violence Prevention Fund
Chapter III
Becoming A Champion, Life Management Success System, People Builders International, Inc., Lexington, S.C.
Chapter V
Love Is A Choice, Recovery for codependent relationships, Dr. Robert Hemfelt, Dr. Frank Minirth, Dr. Paul Meier, Thomas Nelson Publishers, 1989
Learning to Love Yourself, Sharon-Wegscheider-Cruse, Health Communications, Inc., 1987
Chapter VI
Will the Real Women...Please Stand Up!, Ella Patterson, Simon & Schuster, New York, 1996
Self-Renewal, John Gardner, Harper & Row, 1964
Chapter VIII
The Ultimate Woman, Bea Basansky, Tulsa, Oklahoma, 1979
Chapter X
American Legacy, Celebrating African American History and Culture, Spring 2000, Volume 6 / Number 1 Queen Bess: Daredevil Aviator, Doris Rich, Smithsonian Institution Press Washington, D.C., 1993

0-9769645-1-1

NOTES

NOTES

810 232-0018 fc
810 695-5610 res
625-4591 cell

225 E Fifth St
Ste 110
Flt 48502

Printed in the United States
64965LVS00006B/208-234